MITIGATION AND JUSTICE

MITIGATION AND JUSTICE

Where the Truth Meets the Heart of the Story

DERRICK ST. FORT, MSW, CCDI
Founder of Mitigation and Justice

Derrick St. Fort/Evoke180 Publishing

Lauderhill, FL

www.evoke180.com

Printed in the United States of America

Mitigation and Justice: Where The Truth Meets The Heart of The Story/Derrick St. Fort

ISBN 979-8-9884724-6-9   Paperback

TABLE OF CONTENTS

PREFACE

When I started my career almost twenty years ago, I did not know where it would take me, but I knew it had to be better than where I came from. What I came to realize over the years is that although I was successful in my career, where I came from was staring me in the face every day. The clients I serve come from the same type of environments I do. I learned quickly that college degrees and a professional career do nothing to change that.

My success as an investigator and mitigation specialist came with its own set of challenges that triggered anxiety and feelings of imposter syndrome for me. Who was I to be an integral part of saving lives? Lives of people who the world devalues? I refused to let my doubts define me and persevered.

I worked tirelessly and faced every challenge head-on. Rather than succumbing to the stress of being a young professional without guidance, I threw myself into my work, using it as both a distraction and a means of finding my passion. Although this led to a cycle of anxiety and hard work, I found meaning in what I did. Despite professional stagnation and mental exhaustion, I focused my work in criminal justice, knowing that people's lives and futures were in my hands. It was a burden but one that I was proud to carry because I knew I was contributing to my community. To be honest, the anxiety that comes with the work has given me pause many times in my career. I continued to focus my attention on my purpose. My satisfaction is in knowing I am exactly where I need to be in my life, contributing to a community that needs me the most.

This book is a culmination of my experiences, how they shaped me personally and professionally as well as a guide in the areas of investigation and mitigation work. You are about to discover a sub-section of the justice system that is often overlooked. Learn about the foundational elements of investigations, which have remained the same since its inception and the novel approaches and tools that can be used to make them more effective. Whether you are an attorney, investigator, or justice of the court, you will gain valuable insights and skills that can be applied to your practice. If you are a defendant or a family member of someone going through the justice system, you will learn how to assist your attorney and provide effective representation for your loved one. If you are a student, you will gain a deeper under-standing of the fundamental elements of investigations that cannot be learned in the classroom.

This book is the guide that I wish I had when I was starting out as an investigative intern out of college. It provides valuable information and guidance to help you avoid missteps and find your purpose. By dedicating yourself to your purpose and following the steps outlined in this book, you can become more sure, more confident, and more fulfilled.

FOREWORD

The indigent defense work is undeniably challenging, largely due to the emotional investment it necessitates. Dealing with individual lives means grappling directly with their humanity and dignity. The criminal prosecution processes have a knack for stripping both dignity and humanity from those facing criminal charges. From the initial arrest, which erases all privacy, to prolonged stays in unsanitary, unkempt detention facilities during pretrial detention, incarcerated individuals endure a loss of contact with loved ones and the outside world, all before any determination of guilt is made.

Yet, despite progress in the American criminal justice system, a lack of dignity and humanity has persisted since the earliest forms of punishment. Mitigation, often overlooked, is gaining traction as recent shifts in justice systems highlight the importance of delving into the personal histories of criminal defendants. Derrick's advocacy for mitigation and justice sets the stage for a more thoughtful approach within the criminal justice system.

The belief that what you do will have an impact on the outcome is essential. For indigent defenders, the outcome isn't solely about case resolution but about maintaining the dignity and humanity of their clients. Mitigation, through storytelling, is central to achieving this outcome. By artfully narrating their clients' backgrounds, indigent defenders afford them the dignity of understanding their origins. Crucially, clients know their humanity matters to their defense team— no one's worst moments should be considered in isolation.

Thoughtfulness and empathy are indispensable for treating criminal defendants humanely. They ensure decisions about others' lives aren't made rashly but with regard for their ongoing potential. As someone who has practiced criminal law for over a decade, I've seen firsthand how mitigation and thoughtfulness can alter the trajectory of someone's life, regardless of the sentence they receive. Simply listening to someone's story preserves their humanity and dignity.

Too often, offenders spend decades in prison without anyone inquiring about their past, carrying unresolved childhood traumas. This oversight diminishes the progressiveness of our justice system, echoing the harsh practices of the past. Applying methods like those championed by Derrick, wherein mitigation intertwines with the pursuit of justice, can reshape perceptions of the justice system among those familiar with it.

Mitigation, when combined with the pursuit of justice, injects a humane element into the criminal justice system. It sends a message to all offenders that society is interested in understanding the "why." It falls on us, the advocates for the voiceless, to ensure society remains curious about the underlying reasons behind criminal actions.

In the pages of '*Mitigation and Justice*,' we discover that mitigation is justice, reinforcing our dedication to a more equitable and compassionate society—one where every individual's story is heard, understood, and valued.

—Jenna Kelly Esq.

INTRODUCTION

As the end of my junior year at Florida State University drew closer, I realized that I needed to take steps to secure my future. I wanted to find an internship that would provide me with the necessary skills to land a job in criminology after graduation. However, I was not entirely sure what I wanted to do with my life. I decided to meet with my academic advisor and presented her with a list of agencies I had contacted for an internship. Two of them were government agencies, and one was a law office. She looked at the list and suggested one more option, the public 'defender's office. I hesitated at first. Growing up in Liberty City, Miami, I was familiar with the public 'defender's office. It was often the only option for criminal defense representation for people in my community. Unfortunately, the office had a reputation for being the "public pretenders office," which did not make me too enthusiastic about the idea. But something inside me pushed me to take the interview. I arrived at the interview with Chris Elrich, the chief of the Investigator's Unit at the Second Judicial Circuit State Public Defender's Office. Despite my nervousness, Chris put me at ease and made the interview as comfortable as possible. After discussing my background and goals, Chris made a point that stuck with me. He said, "You could intern anywhere you like, but if you decide to work here, you will be working alongside investigators. You will not be shadowing anyone or making coffee for the staff. You will be investigating cases and serving underprivileged people, who are sometimes at the lowest point of their lives." He then raised both palms, saying, "The choice is yours."

His words resonated with me, and later I was reminded that he was making a reference to one of my favorite movies, "*The Matrix*." Like Neo in the movie, I chose the red pill, and my life changed forever. I am forever grateful to Chris for helping me make that decision. May he rest in peace.

I remember vividly the day I started my internship as an investigative intern at the public defender's office. Despite the negative perceptions that surrounded the agency, I decided to commit to the process. I believe that if we want to make a change in society, we have to be a part of the change process. It was a philosophy I believed in and one that had deeply impacted my work. Growing up in a disenfranchised community, I wanted to see changes that would positively affect those like me. I wanted the public defender's office to provide the best quality representation for underserved communities, and I was willing to become a part of the process of change. We cannot allow people's negative perceptions to sway us from our goals. Some of the best attorneys I know have worked for the public defender's office and never received the recognition they deserve. They could have easily moved to private practice, but they stayed committed to their long-term mission of social justice and public service. They did not let others' opinions stop them from fulfilling their purpose.

On my first day, I did not consciously make a decision to commit my life to social justice and public service. It was as if it chose me. As I advanced in my career, I made it my mission to inspire others to be mindful of their abilities and strengths and to use them to help their communities. We all have a part to play in making the world a better place, and if we work together towards our common goal, the conditions of our environment will undoubtedly improve.

CHAPTER ONE:

THE FULL SCOPE

In our daily lives, we often come across situations where we need to use our logical reasoning skills to solve problems. While deductive logic is the most commonly used tool, it is not always enough to arrive at a conclusive solution. Deductive reasoning is a method that involves drawing conclusions based on generally accepted realities. For example, if you order an item online on a Monday and the estimated delivery time is two business days, you would expect to receive it by Wednesday.

On the other hand, inductive reasoning focuses on probability and is used less frequently. For instance, if you live in a neighborhood where package thefts are rampant and your package goes missing after it was reportedly delivered, you may infer that it was stolen. Inductive reasoning requires taking into account past experiences and the context of the situation to arrive at a likely solution.

Abductive reasoning, meanwhile, is a tool that is often employed by investigative professionals to solve problems. This method involves identifying the problem and piecing together clues to arrive at a solution. For example, if you are trying to find a missing package, you may contact the delivery company, question the people you live with, and review security footage to determine what happened. What if you reviewed your security cameras and saw your neighbor approaching your doorstep around the time your package was delivered and leaving with what appears to be your package in their hands? There would be reason to believe that your neighbor "might" be the culprit. By collecting and analyzing all the available evidence, you might be able to deduce what "really" happened.

These problem-solving techniques, or what I call "channeling your inner investigator," involve answering the who, what, when, where, and how questions. Whether it is using deductive reasoning to track a package or employing the other problem-solving methods to investigate an issue, these techniques allow us to arrive at solutions based on the evidence and logic that is right in front of us. They are commonly used in our daily lives, but more complex problems, such as criminal cases, require a more nuanced approach. To arrive at a comprehensive solution, we need to consider the historical contexts, individual characteristics, and other factors that impact the situation.

Refining what I like to call our *"Exceptional Investigator"* skills can better equip us to solve problems that arise. We do not fully get there as professionals by committing to the ancient and simplistic methods. We must continue to develop and refine our skills to become better problem-solvers and improve our overall decision-making abilities so we could have a better perspective of the issue in its entirety so that the appropriate judgment is made.

When we are faced with a problem, it is easy to jump to conclusions and assume the worst without taking the time to gather all the facts. However, as we become more adept at honing in our *"Exceptional Investigator"* skills, we begin to recognize the importance of nuanced thinking while thinking logically. It is essential to consider all the different variables at play and to examine each piece of evidence with an open mind.

In the scenario mentioned earlier, taking the time to search for more answers could have led you to the truth. Rather than assuming that your neighbor stole the package, we could have considered their history and relationship with us. By speaking to them, we could have learned that your neighbor hid the package behind the bushes near your front door to protect it from potential thieves. If we had acted on our initial assumptions and called the police, the situation could have resulted in an arrest that might have been unwarranted.

Unfortunately, instances of wrongful accusations and arrests are all too common. Many police officers rely on outdated investigative techniques that prioritize obtaining quick answers over a thorough investigation. This often leads to the wrongful arrest and conviction of innocent people. It is important to recognize that these injustices affect us all, and we must take steps to address them.

The issue is compounded by the fact that many of these problematic investigative techniques are still being taught in police training programs and other forms of investigative practices. Officers are trained to use buzzwords and other tactics to sustain an arrest, even when they are not warranted. They are encouraged to trample on people's rights and even lie to obtain information.

If we truly want to uncover the truth, then we must work to reform these outdated techniques. By advocating for change and demanding that all agencies including law enforcement prioritize a thorough investigation over a quick resolution, we can help to ensure that justice is served. It is up to all of us to stand up for what is right and demand a more just system for all.

CHAPTER TWO:

HISTORICAL TIMELINE

THE HISTORICAL TIMELINE FROM OLD INVESTIGATIONS TO NEW

The justice system is a complex structure that is all too familiar to the American people. There are two versions of the justice system: one for the rich and one for the poor. Essentially, if you cannot afford adequate representation, then the likelihood of you ending up in jail or prison is high. But what does adequate representation look like? Depending on the case, the defense team should include one or more qualified attorneys, one or more investigators, a paralegal, a legal assistant, and a mitigation specialist. Unfortunately, the right to adequate representation has been under threat since its inception, as most citizens cannot afford the high costs. Historically, the system has been taking its time to fix the problem, and the laws have slowly changed to provide some measure of protection for indigent defendants.

In 1791, the Sixth Amendment was ratified to guarantee a criminal defendant the right to have an attorney defend him or her at trial if the defendant was unable to afford an attorney in a capital case. However, this right was not fully enforced, and many defendants did not have access to competent counsel. It was not until the 1932 case of Powell v. Alabama that the United States Supreme Court reversed the convictions and death sentences of nine African Americans known as the Scottsboro Boys, who were on trial for rape. They met their attorney for the first time during the morning of trial and had no chance to put on a meaningful defense. This shows how the Scottsboro Boys were denied their Sixth Amendment right to effective assistance of counsel because their legal representation was inadequate, and was unable to properly defend them in court. The case made it clear that competent counsel is essential to a fair trial and that defendants who are poor have a right to such counsel.

In 1938, in the Johnson v. Zerbst case, the U.S. Supreme Court ruled that defendants had a right to have counsel appointed at the government's expense if they could not afford to pay for one. This was only afforded to federal cases and was not extended to state courts. The law began to change for indigent defendants in state courts in 1961 when Clarence Earl Gideon was arrested in Panama City, Florida, charged with breaking and entering into the Bay Harbor pool room. He did not have any money for bail nor could he afford an attorney. He was held at the Bay County Jail for two months awaiting trial, and he was found guilty with no attorney, and the judge sentenced him to the maximum of five years in prison. The Supreme Court unanimously extended the rules from the Johnson v. Zerbst case in federal court onto state court cases, allowing indigent clients to have a lawyer if they could not afford one. This was a significant victory for the rights of indigent defendants, although it came almost thirty years after the Johnson v. Zerbst decision. Currently, the Sixth and Fourteenth Amendments guarantee indigent defendants the right to have an attorney appointed, at the government's expense, if they are charged with a serious crime.

The law continued to evolve in the years that followed. In 1972, in the Argersinger v. Hamlin case, the courts extended the Gideon rule to defendants charged with a misdemeanor and facing jail time nearly ten years later. More recently, in the Wiggins v. Smith case in 2003, the U.S. Supreme Court invalidated the death sentence of Kevin Wiggins on the ground that he had ineffective assistance of counsel, in violation of the Sixth Amendment, during the sentencing phase of his trial. The Court based its ruling on the fact that Wiggins's background included childhood abuse, as well as mental illness and borderline intellectual functioning, but defense lawyers did not present such evidence to the jury as mitigating factors that could have prevented the death penalty from being imposed. According to the American Bar Association's 2008 Supplementary Guidelines, the defense team on a capital case should consist of no fewer than two qualified attorneys, an investigator, and a mitigation specialist."

Throughout history, there has been a noticeable trend in the law and investigative practices on how the justice system typically takes a long time to change laws and practices that would benefit its citizens. While the goal of the justice system should be to provide adequate representation, it often falls short in achieving this standard. If adequate representation is the minimum standard, then the gold standard should include the things precisely necessary for each unique case. Judging from history, it may take a while until this becomes mandatory or common practice. It can take many years for changes to be implemented, despite the pressing need for reform.

One significant issue is the slow pace of investigations, which often focus on abductive reasoning without adequately understanding the complexities of the person, their culture, and their upbringing. Without a thorough understanding of these factors, investigations may fail to uncover the necessary information to make a just ruling. Additionally, the justice system tends to overlook systemic and cultural issues that impact individuals as part of an investigation. For example, people in rich areas are often policed differently than those in poor areas. This type of systemic inequality should be taken into account during investigations to better understand the full scope of the person's circumstances.

Furthermore, law enforcement often uses systemic issues as justification for making an arrest instead of using them to understand the person's background and individual characteristics. For instance, law enforcement officers may claim that they have probable cause to search an individual merely because that person was walking around in a "high crime area." Such practices fail to consider the underlying reasons why certain areas are labeled as high crime and how this affects the individuals who live there. They tend to use these systemic issues to make an arrest, instead of using it to understand the full scope of the person's circumstances. Overall, the justice system's tendency to take a long time to change and its failure to understand the cultural complexities of individuals have led to numerous injustices. Reforms are needed to ensure that the justice system can provide adequate representation and investigate cases in a way that fully considers the individual's circumstances and cultural background.

This paragraph highlights a specific incident that exemplifies the issues with law enforcement and the justice system. The incident received national media attention and involved a black male who was walking home from work on a freezing cold night. Despite being engaged in innocent activity, an officer chose to make contact with him, leading to his arrest. This type of misuse of law enforcement discretion challenges the reliability of the officer's decision-making and raises questions about how often this type of encounter happens. While it may have been reasonable for the officer to conduct a welfare check based on the extreme weather, the subsequent actions suggest a problematic trend. This incident underscores the persistence of old practices in police training that perpetuate certain biases, leading to individuals being mistreated. These initial contacts, also known as pretextual stops, often have an ulterior motive to use peaceful interactions with an individual to question them to see "if they were up to no good."

The incident demonstrates the slow pace at which the justice system changes to better serve its citizens. There have been numerous instances where the police use pretextual stops to investigate a person further, leading to unlawful arrests and violations of rights. Despite these well-documented issues, little has changed, and these practices persist. This is not an attack on police encounters, it is simply an attack on the systemic and cultural issues that contribute to the mistreatment of individuals by law enforcement and old practices that persist in training. The failure to address these issues leads to a culture where individuals are treated unfairly and certain groups are disproportionately targeted. The justice system needs to understand the cultural complexities of a person, their upbringing, and individual characteristics that they have developed over time to conduct a proper investigation. Without a deep understanding of these factors, justice cannot be served, and the justice system will continue to struggle to make significant change with the times.

CHAPTER THREE:

THE CULTURE OF INVESTIGATIONS

Discretion has been misused in investigations, where the investigator would not take the time to consider all the information. This leads to arrests where people were wrongfully convicted. Wrongful arrests, also known as false arrests, are a serious problem in the United States. Unfortunately, it is difficult to determine an exact statistic on wrongful arrests because many cases are not reported or are not documented in a way that can be easily tracked.

A report from the National Institute of Justice estimates that approximately ten thousand people are wrongfully convicted of serious crimes each year in the United States (Wrongful Convictions, n.d.) This includes cases where individuals were wrongfully arrested and later convicted. While there is no definitive statistic on the number of wrongful arrests in the United States, the available data of overturned convictions suggests a high number of innocent people are arrested and/or convicted.

The number of wrongful convictions indicates that we need to evaluate how to properly collect facts and investigate cases. I propose that we start creating change by evaluating current training models. Later in the chapter, I will share some things to consider on how to create more effective practices in investigations. Before I do that, I would like to explore "the investigator." Who is the investigator? What does the investigator do?

When it comes to complex issues that require in-depth knowledge and expertise, seeking the assistance of a professional investigator is often the best course of action. From tracing missing packages to representing clients in criminal defense cases, investigators are well-equipped to tackle a wide range of challenges. In fact, there are countless situations where we may feel compelled to channel our "inner investigator" in order to uncover the truth. But once you have exhausted all of your options, then the next course of action should be to reach out to a professional.

For instance, when suspicions arise regarding infidelity in a relationship, many individuals find themselves consumed with the need to get to the bottom of things. In such cases, a private investigator can provide a sense of clarity and closure by conducting discreet surveillance and gathering relevant evidence. Similarly, in business settings, investigators can be invaluable assets in uncovering instances of fraud or embezzlement.

Regardless of the specific circumstances, the common thread among those who seek out the services of a professional investigator is the desire to solve a problem. Whether it means sifting through a mountain of data or conducting interviews with potential witnesses, investigators are skilled at putting together the puzzle pieces of information to create a comprehensive picture of any given situation. The expertise of a professional investigator allows clients to feel confident that their issues will be resolved in the most efficient and effective manner possible.

Take a minute to think about the image of the investigator that you are channeling. When we think about investigators, we often imagine a caricatured figure from a sensationalized television show or movie, like a Dick Tracy or Sherlock Holmes, dressed in a dark trench coat, holding a magnifying glass. Or it could likely resemble the more modern TV shows like *Law and Order* or *CSI*. The images have clearly changed over time; however, the investigative techniques remained the same. These images are often outdated and no longer reflect the reality of what most investigators look like today. In fact, investigators come from all walks of life, and they do not have to fit the mold of a typical sleuth in order to be successful. Rather than trying to conform to an image that does not fit, it is important to appreciate your own unique qualities and use them to your advantage.

This is especially true when it comes to investigative techniques. While there are certainly some techniques that have stood the test of time, others are in need of revision. In particular, many of the methods used in the past relied heavily on outdated technology and tools that are no longer as effective. Today's investigators need to be equipped with the latest tools and techniques in order to stay ahead of the game. That means staying up-to-date on the latest resources that can aid in the investigative process.

It is important not to lose sight of the *human* element of investigation. The deductive, abductive, or inductive reasoning skills that could be powerful can also be misleading or unreliable. It is important for investigators to have a deep understanding of human behavior, as well as the ability to connect with people from all walks of life. By combining both of these elements, investigators can provide their clients with the most effective and comprehensive services possible.

In short, the image of the investigator as a trench-coat-wearing, magnifying-glass-wielding sleuth may be a thing of the past, but the need for investigative services is more important than ever. We must stay grounded by embracing the realities of human behavior, so we could provide our clients with the best possible outcomes. It creates the avenue to help tell a client's story from a unique investigative perspective.

When we think of detective shows, we often picture gripping dramas with high stakes and shocking plot twists. However, what many people do not realize is that these shows often focus on drama rather than the actual investigative process. In fact, most of these shows only show a small fraction of what an investigation actually entails. They often rely on a single piece of evidence to solve the entire case, which is not an accurate representation of the real-life complexities of solving crimes.

Moreover, these shows often fail to highlight the various roles that investigators play in a case. There are many different types of investigators beyond those who work for the police or sheriff's departments, and each type of investigator has a unique set of skills and responsibilities. Additionally, these shows rarely explore the steps that individuals take to become investigators, which can be a complex and challenging process depending on the field of investigations.

The images portrayed on television do not accurately represent the majority of investigators in the field. In order for the best and brightest individuals to join and excel in this industry, they must have access to the most innovative methods and technologies available. This includes access to information and educational tools that can help them develop the skills they need to succeed. By providing more opportunities for education and training, we can inspire more people to pursue careers in investigation and create a more diverse and effective field.

While detective shows may be entertaining, they do not accurately represent the realities of investigation. By shining a light on the many roles that investigators play and the steps they take to become experts in their field, we can help people better understand the complexities of solving crimes. Furthermore, we can inspire more people to pursue careers in investigation and drive innovation in the field.

To increase awareness and understanding of the investigative field, it is crucial for the public to be exposed to the various types of investigators and their respective roles. Educating the public on this important aspect of the justice system will encourage more people to contribute to the industry.

In the past, investigators were known for their discreetness, but in today's world, it is important for them to be more visible and accessible to the public. One way to achieve this is by creating opportunities for investigators to take on roles as educators. They can participate in presentations, podcasts, docuseries, and other forums to share their knowledge and experience. By doing so, investigators can help reshape the image of what investigators truly look like and what their work entails.

The best investigators are those who understand the foundation of their field, while also being inspired to go beyond the basics. These individuals I referred to as *"Exceptional Investigators"* constantly strive to improve their skills, knowledge, and expertise. Through education and public outreach, investigators can inspire the next generation of *"Exceptional Investigators"* and continue to push the field forward.

CHAPTER FOUR:

THE *EXCEPTIONAL INVESTIGATOR*

AUTHENTICITY

We must shatter the thoughts and images of who we believe an investigator should be. Authenticity is crucial in the field of investigations, as it involves shattering the preconceived notion of what the community thinks an investigator should look like. This includes shedding the televised image of arrogance and adopting a unique set of skills that drive one's investigative personality. It is important to know who you are and to be genuine in that professional space. While exploring different styles is acceptable, it is essential to avoid styles that pull you away from who you are. The lesson that I have learned from attempting to replicate the investigative styles of others is that being true to yourself is crucial. It is okay to explore different styles, but remember, the community can quickly spot insincerities, which could harm the reputation of an investigator. Being genuine in this profession leads to self-confidence, making it a skill transferable to any job.

TAKE A CLOSER LOOK

Taking the extra step in your case investigations is crucial. Merely gathering information is not enough. Dispelling doubt should be the focal point throughout your investigations and must be addressed to complete the job. For instance, if you were uncertain whether you turned off the stove before going to bed, your investigative instincts should prompt you to check it to remove any lingering doubt even though the court standard is "*beyond a reasonable doubt.*" Guesswork would not suffice, particularly when the necessary information is readily available. Using basic solution-focused skills is an approach that investigators should employ regularly. Identifying the who, what, when, where, why and how should be second nature to investigators. It is also equally important to understand the context of the case as a whole. Going beyond the basic facts to understand the broader picture is vital to solving the case effectively. By taking the extra step to uncover the truth and investigate the case thoroughly, investigators can ensure that they are doing their job on an elite level.

IT IS OKAY NOT TO HAVE ALL THE ANSWERS

It is essential to understand that you will not have all the answers and solve every case as an investigator, and that's perfectly okay. What matters most is that you follow through with your problem-solving techniques. Being willing to learn and taking the extra steps necessary to identify the multidimensional complexities of an individual, their circumstances, and the community they live in, is a hallmark of an "Exceptional Investigator." These investigators continuously follow up with continuing education and polishing their investigative techniques to excel in their profession. If an investigator does not understand an issue in a case, they take the extra step to educate themselves about the topic before doing any work on it. They may also confer with a colleague to gain a sense of how they approached a similar issue. Admitting when you do not have all the answers and seeking out the knowledge to solve the problem is a valuable skill for investigators. With perseverance and dedication, even the most challenging cases can be solved.

HAVE A THEORETICAL FRAMEWORK

In order to become an "Exceptional Investigator", you should practice under a theoretical framework. A theoretical framework is usually a series of studied perspectives that is ordinarily used in a person's daily profession. It affects the way they examine subjects and serve as a roadmap to addressing issues on constructing resolutions. There should be a framework that centers your practice. Your framework should be rooted in scientific principles to assist you in making knowledgeable investigative decisions, as opposed to trial, error, and repeat. It provides you with consistency, reliability, and a means to avoid recreating the wheel.

SOLUTION-FOCUSED FRAMEWORK

One of the theoretical orientations that I find useful is the modernized version of the Solution-Focused Brief Theory. "SFBT is a short-term, goal-oriented approach that works with a [client's] strengths, to help them create the future [they] desire" (Moore and Casabianca, 2022). There is a professional and client relationship in criminal cases. As an investigator, attorney, or justice of the court, the focus is to find out what is important to the client, how they believe their life would be if their challenges were resolved and what strengths they have to make it happen. This approach allows the client to have autonomy on making the important decision in their case and in their personal lives. "The goal of SFBT is to help clients see the tools that they have access to, that they would not normally see in their lives. The tools and the skills that [the clients] have, may help [them] change harmful behaviors, achieve lifelong goals and manage difficult situations" (Moore and Casabianca, 2022). This theoretical framework allows you, the professional, to help resolve problems that the client determines to be an issue. Ultimately, it is the client's choice whether they want to go to trial or not. It is the client's choice, whether they want treatment for substance abuse or not. They make the decisions. Empowering the client to make those decisions would build a level of respect, admiration, and appreciation. There was a systematic review of thirty-three studies in 2017 that found that strength and resource oriented SFBT techniques were effective for the diverse challenges they were used for (Moore and Casabianca, 2022). SFBT is not only a theory; it's backed by research as well.

CLIENT CENTERED THEORY

Utilizing Client Centered Theory as a framework in criminal defense can provide several benefits. It is one of the hallmarks of the social work profession since its inception. Client Centered Theory is based on the belief that a person's innate self-actualizing tendencies would flourish if the environment were conducive to growth. This theory places the focus on how the environment drastically affects a person's decision-making.

For instance, a person raised in poor conditions may have a higher propensity for theft as a means of survival, compared to someone from a middle-class household who always had all their needs met. This puts the locus of change in the environment. From their perspective, it is the environment that adapts rather than the people. By applying Client Centered Theory to criminal defense, lawyers, investigators, and other professionals can work to identify and address the environmental factors that may have contributed to their clients' actions. This approach takes into account the individual circumstances of each case and seeks to provide a more holistic and personalized defense strategy. Additionally, it recognizes the need for ongoing support and intervention to help clients overcome the underlying challenges they may be facing. Utilizing Client Centered Theory in criminal defense can help to promote greater understanding and empathy towards clients, while also working towards a more just and equitable legal system.

According to Turner (1996), Carl Rogers, the creator of Client Centered Theory (CCT), believed that humans have a natural inclination towards growth and fulfilling their potential. According to his theory, individuals are inherently positive and will thrive if accepted for who they are without being forced into societal expectations. The core concept of CCT is to look at the individual and determine the root cause of their problems. By understanding the individual's unique circumstances and experiences, professionals can help them reach their full potential and live a fulfilling life.

The principles of CCT can also be applied to criminal defense cases, where understanding the individual's background and motivations can be crucial. By taking a client-centered approach, members of the defense team can better advocate for their clients and build strong cases. This involves listening to the client's perspective, considering their unique circumstances, and working towards a positive outcome that benefits both the client and society as a whole. By utilizing the principles of CCT, attorneys, investigators and mitigation specialists can help clients overcome the challenges they face and move forward towards a better future. The justice system as a whole, including probation officers and prosecutors, could benefit from utilizing principles of CCT to improve our society. The following is a list of tools utilized in CCT (Turner, 1996) p. 80).

1. Establishing rapport

2. Reflecting client experiences

3. Self-Disclosure

4. Treating client as a unique individual

5. Actively Listening

6. Empathizing accurately

7. Challenging

8. Sharing an authentic relationship

9. Interpreting if appropriate

10. Encouraging healthy lifestyle changes

In my application of CCT, when I meet with a client, I initially introduce myself and define my role within the relationship. I set ground rules and expectations for both myself and the client. I hear the client's goals and provide clear and precise short-term and long-term goals that I will attempt to achieve with the client's help. I always say what I mean and mean what I say. If I say that I will do something, I will do my best to get it done. If I am not able to, then I will explain why as soon as the opportunity presents itself. I focus on the client as a person rather than focusing only on the problem. I try to be as transparent as possible and keep them included in all the decisions made involving their case. I challenge them, when necessary, to attain fully accurate information. Finally, I provide the client with all the options available to allow them to make the best decisions for themselves.

Many of the values that are expressed in CCT are fundamental to the social work practice (Turner, 1996, p. 77). The National Association of Social Workers' (NASW) core values exemplify how the approach to investigations can be if we shift the culture of investigations. Below is the list of core values.

Service: To help people in need and address social problems.

- To elevate service to others above self-interest. To draw on their knowledge, values, and skills to help people in need and to address social problems. To be encouraged to volunteer some portion of their professional skills with no expectation of significant financial return (pro bono service).

Social Justice: To challenge social injustice.

- To pursue social change, particularly with and on behalf of vulnerable and oppressed individuals and groups of people. Social change efforts are focused primarily on issues of poverty, unemployment, discrimination, and other forms of social injustice. These activities seek to promote sensitivity to and knowledge about oppression as well as cultural and ethnic diversity. We strive to ensure access to needed information, services, and resources; equality of opportunity; and meaningful participation in decision making for all people.

Dignity and Worth of the Person: To respect the inherent dignity and worth of the person.

- To treat each person in a caring and respectful fashion, mindful of individual differences and cultural and ethnic diversity. To promote clients' socially responsible self-determination. Social workers seek to enhance clients' capacity and opportunity to change and to address their own needs. We are cognizant of their dual responsibility to clients and to the broader society. They seek to resolve conflicts between clients' interests and the broader society's interests in a socially responsible manner consistent with the values, ethical principles, and ethical standards of the profession.

Importance of Human Relationships: To recognize the central importance of human relationships.
- To understand that relationships between and among people are an important vehicle for change. To engage people as partners in the helping process. Seeking to strengthen relationships among people in a purposeful effort to promote, restore, maintain, and enhance the well-being of individuals, families, social groups, organizations, and communities.

Integrity: To behave in a trustworthy manner.
- To be continually aware of the profession's mission, values, ethical principles, and ethical standards and practice in a manner consistent with them. To take measures to care for themselves professionally and personally. To act honestly and responsibly and promote ethical practices on the part of the organizations with which they are affiliated.

Competence: To practice within their areas of competence and develop and enhance their professional expertise.
- To continually strive to increase their professional knowledge and skills and to apply them in practice. We should aspire to contribute to the knowledge base of the profession.

CONTINUED EDUCATION

To become an *Exceptional Investigator*, it is important to not only focus on your own investigative practices but also to stay informed about developments in related fields. This can involve reading articles, purchasing books, and attending seminars and conferences. By doing so, you can refine your skills and build relationships with other professionals in your community. This can be instrumental in developing valuable contacts and enhancing your career trajectory.

Continued education is also crucial for success in the field of investigation. By dedicating time and effort to purchasing literature and attending educational courses, you can refine your skills and develop a niche or area of expertise. These added skills will set you apart from others and may even provide additional income streams. For example, after years of working as a criminal defense investigator, I decided to pursue a master's degree in social work. The skills I acquired from my MSW degree provided me with a wider range of opportunities and allowed me to refine my investigative approach with a more holistic and empathetic perspective. As a result, I was able to expand my capabilities and take on more diverse cases, ultimately improving my effectiveness as an investigator.

UNDERSTANDING YOUR ROLE

The first step in any investigative role is to understand your specific responsibilities and limitations. Some investigators are given specific tasks to complete, while others have more flexibility to explore various avenues related to a case. The role you play can vary greatly from case to case and even within the same case. For example, you may be tasked with delivering certified documents to an individual in one instance, while in another case, you may be asked to complete a comprehensive investigation that involves fact-finding, witness interviews, trial preparation, and mitigation work. It is crucial to have a clear understanding of your role as an investigator in each situation to ensure you are meeting the expectations of your client and the agency you work for.

This book will explore various investigative techniques and strategies to help you become a more effective investigator. Additionally, it will provide you with more resources and information to further your understanding of these specific methods. By having a strong grasp of your role and utilizing proven techniques and resources, you can become a successful investigator who delivers results for your clients or employer.

It is time to move beyond the basic and outdated line of questioning that has been the norm for far too long. This traditional approach to investigations overlooks the unique qualities of each individual and their specific circumstances. The practice of investigation has remained largely unchanged since its inception, and it's time for a new approach. Collecting facts alone is no longer enough. Modern criminal investigations require a transformative approach that considers the different aspects of all parties involved. This approach is similar to the principles and core values of the Client-Centered Theory and the National Association of Social Workers principles. By adopting a more comprehensive and nuanced approach to investigations, we can better understand the individuals and circumstances involved in a case. This not only leads to more effective investigations, but it also promotes greater justice and equity. It is time to embrace a new way of investigating, one that prioritizes the needs and unique qualities of each individual involved.

CHAPTER FIVE:

EXPLORING DIFFERENT TYPES OF INVESTIGATORS

In this section of the book, we will explore the various paths to becoming a fact finder and discuss the steps you can take to work in this industry. We will also explore fields that offer investigator positions, which are often overlooked. However, before we dive in, it is essential to address some of the biggest misconceptions that people have about being an investigator.

One of the most common misconceptions is that a college degree is required to become an investigator. This is not entirely true. Although a college degree or additional educational or training certificates can improve your chances of being hired, having a high school diploma is often the minimum requirement. In fact, experience and other certifications can sometimes be substituted for a college degree.

Another misconception is that you must have a degree in criminal justice to work in this field. This is also not entirely true. There are many professionals in this industry with degrees and backgrounds in diverse fields, such as English majors, former practicing attorneys, and even those with a high school diploma. It is important to utilize the uniqueness of your background to your advantage. For example, if you have an English degree, you could pursue a career as an investigative journalist or a criminal defense investigator, which requires a lot of writing skills to articulate information from dialogues, records, and observations.

The misconception that all investigators wear uniforms or shirts and ties is also far from the truth. The dress code depends on your field of interest. For instance, those attending court proceedings regularly need to dress professionally. But there are private investigators who work undercover and have to dress like civilians to blend in with the population. Also, investigators in the field of computer forensics spend most of their time examining electronics and do not necessarily need to dress professionally.

Another misconception is that investigators must memorize all the laws. In reality, it is impossible to memorize every single law. However, it is vital to at least review the laws that govern your practice. It is best to review them seasonally to hold yourself accountable and make the information easier to absorb. If you come across a law related to your practice, add it to your list of noted laws, to be able to go back to it quickly when needed. Nowadays, it is not necessary to memorize all laws since information is easily accessible on the internet.

Lastly, many people believe that you must possess a license to become an investigator, but this is not always the case. In Florida, for example, Chapter 493 of the Florida Statutes regulates the security industry, private investigative industry, and recovery agency industry. It explains who is exempt from licensing. If you are from another state, refer to the governing body that oversees private investigations.

WHO IS EXEMPT FROM LICENSING
(Florida Department of Agriculture and Consumer Services, n.d.)

- "In-house" recovery agents, unarmed security officers, and private investigators who are solely, exclusively, and regularly employed in connection with the business of the employer when an employer-employee relationship exists is exempt from licensing.
- Any insurance investigator or adjuster licensed by a state or federal licensing authority when such a person is providing expert advice within the scope of her or his license.
- Any individual solely, exclusively, and regularly employed as an unarmed investigator in connection with the business of her or his employer, when there exists an employer-employee

relationship.
- Any attorney in the regular practice of her or his profession.
- Any person who holds a professional license under the laws of this state when such person is providing services or expert advice in the profession or occupation in which that person is so licensed.
- Any private investigative agency, and employees thereof, performing contractual investigative services solely and exclusively for any agency of the United States.
- Any person duly authorized by the laws of this state to operate a central burglar or fire alarm business. However, such persons are not exempt to the extent they perform services requiring licensure or registration under this chapter.

The private investigator (PI) license is not required for staff investigators in various professions such as investigative insurance adjusters, child protective investigators, investigators for the state attorney's office, investigators employed by the public defender's office, investigators who work for the IRS, and more. However, obtaining a PI license can be highly beneficial for staff investigators. It can improve their credibility with clients, colleagues, and employers, as it indicates that the investigator has undergone proper training and passed the necessary exams. It demonstrates that they possess the knowledge and skills required to conduct professional investigations. Having a PI license could also provide networking opportunities with other investigators and professionals in the field, which can help you stay up-to-date with the latest trends, techniques, and best practices. Many professional organizations and associations require members to hold a PI license, so obtaining one could open doors to join these organizations and stay connected with others in the industry. Another significant reason to obtain a PI license is that it can broaden career options and provide a backup plan for staff investigators. Holding a PI license can enable staff investigators to expand into other industries and even start their own businesses.

If you are interested in a career in investigations, it is important to identify which type of investigations you are interested in and take the necessary steps to pursue it. Consider your interests and skills to find the area of investigations that aligns with your strengths. Some areas may require a specific skill set, such as expertise in accounting or a background in social work. There are many different fields of investigation, each with their own unique focus and skill set. For example, some professionals focus on financial investigations, while others may work in child welfare or family law. Before choosing a specific field, take the time to research and learn about the different types of cases they typically handle. This can help you narrow down your options and find an area that you are passionate about. Networking with professionals in your desired field can also provide valuable insight and advice. Reaching out to people who are currently working in the field and asking them about their experiences. They may be able to offer guidance on ways to get started and what it takes to succeed in the industry. Additionally, gaining hands-on experience through internships or volunteering can be incredibly helpful. This can provide valuable training and skills that will carry over to your future career. It can also help you determine if a particular field is a good fit for you. Taking the time to research and gain experience in the field can help you make an informed decision and pursue a career that is rewarding and fulfilling.

CHILD WELFARE INVESTIGATIONS

If you have a passion for child welfare, you may consider becoming a child protective investigator. A bachelor's degree in a related field, such as criminology, criminal justice, or social work is generally required, along with additional certifications on topics related to child welfare from the Florida certification board. In addition, you must have a valid driver's license and an operational vehicle to perform daily work activities, including traveling to a child's home or school to check on their well-being. Transportation is a must in this industry.

MEDIA

If you are interested in media, you could consider being an investigative journalist or a reporter. Employers in larger markets, like news channels, typically require some experience, but do not let that discourage you. Today's social media climate provides an opportunity to create your own investigative reporting and grow a following, which can make you more attractive to larger market companies. A college degree in communications, journalism, or a related field is usually preferred, but exceptions can be made based on experience. Although there are no licensing requirements because of the First Amendment's freedom of the press, affiliating with organizations like the Florida Center for Investigative Reporting can provide a foundation and a way to practice ethically in the field. These organizations offer training on ethics and fact-checking sources to ensure accurate and truthful reporting while maintaining objectivity and avoiding personal biases that may influence reporting.

FINANCIAL INVESTIGATIONS

If you are interested in working on financial crimes, you may consider working with the IRS. These investigations usually involve investigating fraud, embezzlement, or other illegal activities. To qualify, you must be a U.S. citizen, at least twenty-one years old upon completing the training academy and no older than thirty-seven at time of appointment. Although specific experience or educational background is not mentioned, qualifications are based on education, specialized experience, or a combination of both. You must also possess a valid driver's license, pass a background check, a pre-employment medical exam, a pre-employment drug test, and a pre-employment tax examination, and be legally allowed to carry a firearm. Having some experience in business or accounting would also be helpful. Contrary to popular belief, you do not have to become a law enforcement officer first to pursue government jobs like this. Do your research and take steps towards reaching your goal.

CRIMINAL DEFENSE INVESTIGATION

If you are interested in criminal law, you may consider working in criminal investigations. Although most people believe investigations are conducted only by law enforcement agencies, there are several routes you can take to focus on solving crimes, identifying witnesses, and gathering evidence. With a high school degree, you could volunteer with your local public defender's office as an investigative intern. Qualifications vary, but at a minimum, you must have a high school diploma. If you are a college student, you could also commit to an internship to gain experience. This not only provides the skills to perform investigative duties but also an opportunity to be hired as a staff member. You do not need many qualifications to volunteer or intern; all that is required is your time and commitment to public service. As a criminal defense investigator, you can gather information about individuals, organizations, and crimes from a defense perspective. Another option is to become a private investigator, for which you would need to acquire a private investigator license. Please review the chart for details on acquiring your license in Florida.

Chart A

Additional Requirements to Become a PI

In the state of Florida, you must acquire a private investigator license if you intend on conducting private investigations as detailed in Chapter 493 in the Florida Statutes.

Here is the process of obtaining a PI license in the state of Florida, which varies from state to state. According to Chapter 493, you must be at least eighteen years old. You must be a legal resident. You must have good moral character and provide references of people who have known you to practice good judgment. **You must not have a disqualifying criminal record as detailed in chapter 493 (See Reference table—Graphic: guilty of or had an adjudication withheld for related crimes not limited to the following: trespassing, breaking and entering, burglary, robbery, forgery, criminal mischief or theft, assault, battery, stalking, aggravated battery, aggravated assault, sexual battery, kidnapping, armed robbery, murder, aggravated stalking, resisting an officer with violence).** You must have two years of lawfully gained, verifiable, full-time experience. Examples of experience include, private investigative work or related fields of work that provided equivalent experience or training. College coursework related to criminal justice, criminology, or law enforcement administration, or successful completion of any law-enforcement-related training received from any federal, state, county, or municipal agency, except that no more than one year may be used from this category. There are special provisions and accommodations for veterans. Please refer to chapter 493 of the Florida Statutes for more information.

For internships doing private investigation, interns must acquire a Class "CC" license. This internship must be done at a licensed private investigative agency.

The next step is to pass the Florida private investigator license exam which simply covers chapter 493 in its entirety and deals with the private investigator industry. The exam consists of one hundred multiple choice questions which takes about two hours to complete. Once you have passed the exam, you could apply and submit an application for your CC or C license. A Class CC is a licensed internship, and a Class C is an official private investigator license. You would then need to get physical fingerprints from a police or sheriff's department to include with your application.

Chart B

Key Regulations to Consider as a Private Investigator

The private investigator C and CC license allows you to work for a private investigator business.

You cannot perform investigations if you are not practicing under a private investigator A licensed business. According to Chapter 493 in the Florida Statutes, any person, firm, company, partnership, or corporation that engages in business as a private investigative agency must have a Class "A" license.

So, there are two options. You could attain your C license and search for a licensed investigative firm to work under. It is important for the investigative firm you work under to hold an "A" investigative license.

You can also fill out a class "A" application to get your private investigator business license and your C license simultaneously. The applications are readily available on the Department of Agriculture and Consumer Services website.

The Department also requires you to submit a color photo like a passport photograph, which will be the image they use on your identification card. If you are submitting both the A and C license together, then you are only required to submit one set of fingerprints and pay one fingerprint processing fee. You must renew your class C license every two years and your class A license every three years.

Obtaining a private investigator license enables you to perform a broad range of investigative and security tasks in the private sector, encompassing but not limited to the following:

- Accident investigations
- Asset locates
- Background checks
- Capital murder cases
- Child custody/Child support investigations
- Civil/ Wrongful deaths cases
- Cybercrimes
- Corporate investigations
- Criminal investigations
- Electronic forensics
- Financial/Fraud investigations
- Infidelity investigations
- Mitigation in criminal defense
- Missing persons/skip traces searches
- Process service

SUMMARY

In the state of Florida, you could work as an in-house legal investigator for a law firm without a private investigator license. Remember, you must be an employee for that law firm. For example, the public defender's office is a law firm, and they employ in-house staff investigators and investigative interns. These investigators are able to practice investigations without a license because they work for that law office. However, if you are an independent contractor, practicing as an investigator, and you do contract work for law offices, businesses, or people in the United States, you must acquire a private investigator license. In the state of Florida, it is illegal to do private investigator work without a license. Please review chart A and Chapter 493 of the Florida Statutes concerning the penalties and general updates.

CHAPTER SIX

CREATING SUCCESS: TIPS FOR BEING AN EFFECTIVE INVESTIGATOR

GET A MENTOR

Once you have narrowed the field that you are interested in, you should consider acquiring a mentor, a person who you could reach out to, who has experience in the field. A mentor could provide guidance and support to help you navigate your career path and offer advice on important career decisions in your life. They could help you set goals, objectives, and provide insight into the industry. They could also hold you accountable to those goals and objectives to ensure that you stay on track and focused on achieving them. A mentor could also introduce you to other professionals in the field, expanding your network and providing you with access to new opportunities. They could help talk you through complex investigative questions you may have. Most importantly, they could offer training and other professional development opportunities. If you have the right mentor, they will share their expertise and experiences and provide constructive feedback to help you improve.

Having the opportunity to listen to an experienced mentor could help you avoid making mistakes in your career. We have all been in situations where we felt stagnant and sometimes burned out. Mentors often help with providing a fresh perspective on your work and bring your attention to opportunities outside of the workspace. Having a mentor is incredibly valuable for career development and professional growth. There is nothing like building your skills, expanding your network, and receiving support along the way. If an opportunity arises, they would be able to write letters of recommendation on your behalf. I currently have about twenty mentees who reach out from time to time. I am proud to say that each of them is successfully employed in the criminology or social work profession through my guidance. I appreciate witnessing the growth in my mentees. Our professional relationship has grown to where I no longer see them as my mentees but my peers in the field of investigations. They are a part of my professional community and we support each other.

GET EXPERIENCE

Before filling out an application, before making official steps towards your profession, you should consider obtaining experience in that field of interest first. Internships and volunteering opportunities could provide you with hands-on experience in the field, allowing you to build relevant skills that would be valuable in your future career. It could also help you determine which specific area in the field that most interests you. If you commit to an internship and later decide that you are no longer interested in the field, at the end of your internship you could choose to work somewhere else. Remember, the experience that you acquired could be useful for another job, or future career opportunities.

Professions within the justice system can be intense and demanding. Internships could expose you to real-world scenarios and allow you to gain a better understanding of what it is like to work in the field, including the challenges and rewards from your hard work. It could help you develop important personal qualities such as teamwork, communication and leadership skills, which are essential in any career. Amongst everything else, an internship could help you build your professional network. This is how most people encounter their first professional mentor. Most people do not have access to people in the field unless they have worked in the field. Internships and volunteering could provide you access to not only a mentor but to valuable connections and potential job opportunities in the future. When I started my first internship at the public defender's office, it provided me with opportunities to meet and work with other professionals like, social workers, private attorneys, judges, and so on...relationships that I still maintain till this day.

Starting an internship helps you build a foundation through valuable work experience and helps you build the relevant skills necessary for your field. In my opinion, working with the public defender's office is a valuable experience. The public defenders offices are often responsible for representing clients who may not be able to afford legal representation. By interning there, you have an opportunity to contribute to social justice efforts by providing legal assistance to those who need it the most. It helps you build compassion for people who are at times, going through the lowest point of their lives. It would help you gain a deeper understanding of the legal system and how it affects people like you and me. The public defender's office usually offers internships and positions to volunteers year-round. I personally feel that we are morally obligated to contribute to society through public service and social justice efforts in our communities.

When I started my internship, I had the opportunity to gain experience with various criminal cases such as family court, drug court, juvenile cases, traffic cases, passing worthless bank check cases, misdemeanor cases, felony cases, and capital murder cases. Each of these divisions is unique and could potentially be your niche population of interest in the future.

Because the public defender's office has so many cases, you would have the opportunity to assist line investigators with their caseload. This would usually include interviewing defendants, interviewing witnesses, requesting for records, taking photographs of the crime scene, serving subpoenas, contributing to defense strategy, possibly testifying in court, and the list goes on. If this position is not available, feel free to intern or volunteer at any government agency or a private attorney firm.

During your internship, you should put forth maximum effort into learning various investigative skills and specializing focus on case-related tasks to attain positive outcomes. Socialize with your coworkers, supervisors, and other legal professionals to build rapport and your professional network. This network could be helpful in finding future job opportunities. There is nothing like leaving a lasting impression at your internship. That would definitely give you a leg up with your work experience, and the possibility to be hired as a young professional. The work is uniquely satisfying and could pave the way to your future career.

CHAPTER SEVEN:

THE ART OF MITIGATION

I am fueled by an unwavering dedication to public service and the fight for social justice. My passion and commitment have led me to the public defender's office—a natural fit for someone who refuses to turn a blind eye to injustice. Through my employment, I gained a profound understanding of the justice system and the people I served. My clients were more than just cases to me. They were a reflection of myself and the people I hold dear. I saw my cousins, uncles, and friends in their struggles. It became clear to me that their situations could easily be mine. A single misstep or the wrong choice could have landed me in their shoes. I can vividly recall all the negative interactions I have had with law enforcement, and I shudder at the thought of what could have happened if the officer misused their discretion. These experiences drive me to be an advocate for change, to work tirelessly towards a future where every person is treated with fairness and respect, regardless of their background or circumstances.

The truth is clear...Our justice system is fundamentally lopsided. It is evident when you look at the budgets of government agencies—the police, the sheriff, and the prosecution receive the lion's share of funding while the public defender's office is left severely under-funded and unable to compensate their employees properly. In fact, the most recent budget figures speak volumes. In 2022, the Orlando police department received a staggering $210 million dollars, which is a 7.5 percent increase from the previous year. This means that the police department alone has 30.5 percent of the city's budget. Meanwhile, public service agencies only received a mere 1.7 percent of the budget, as per the General Fund Expenditures from the city of Orlando.

Turning our attention to the Orange County Recommended Budget for the Fiscal Year 2021–2022, we can see that the district attorney was allotted $166,624,429, while the sheriff court operations received $51,036,148. The probation office was given $194,405,696, and the sheriff-coroner received a staggering $775,503,427. The trial courts received $66,725,899. All of these agencies combined sustain a budget to focus solely on one aspect of a client's life, their criminal charges. This does not even include the money allotted for special task forces given to law enforcement agencies and civil forfeitures.

What about the public defender's office, the only line of defense for clients who cannot afford legal representation? They are given $89,741,469, which is a paltry amount compared to what the prosecution receives. This disparity in funding for client representation in criminal court causes hard-working employees to feel stuck and unappreciated. It is no surprise that the community looks down on the public defender's office, wondering how they can possibly handle the overwhelming number of cases with so little support.

It is time to acknowledge that the justice system is failing those who need it most. The severely underfunded public defender's office stretches to provide the best services with low funding. However, the truth is without sufficient capital, the public defender's office will not be able to provide adequate representation for clients who cannot afford it, while law enforcement and prosecution agencies receive overwhelming amounts of funding. This is an injustice that cannot be ignored, and it is time for change.

Working at the public defender's office can be challenging, to say the least. As an investigator, I was constantly faced with the lack of resources that made it difficult to contribute more. Motivating myself was an uphill task, with no one to provide the necessary guidance. I stayed because I loved the work and knew that it was important.

To survive in such a field, you must be self-motivated. Kendra Cherry's theory on self-determination and motivation rings true. The belief that what you do will have an impact on the outcome is essential. So, I set small goals for myself, which led to me earning a master's degree in social work. I was determined to fill a void I had felt for a long time.

I started researching and reading literature on other fields in the criminal justice system including books on law enforcement. However, the thought of arresting someone made me uncomfortable. I then stumbled upon the field of bail bonds, but it was not for me. I could not bring myself to get paid or to get access to a defendant's assets while they are in the lowest time in their life. Many times, defendants are desperate to be bailed out of jail and do not have the funds to post their own bail, leading them to call on a bail bondsman who has a direct financial gain in the criminal justice system.

Working at the public defender's office requires self-motivation, re-silience, and a genuine love for the job. It is not for everyone, but for those who choose to stay, it is a rewarding experience. Creating a healthy environment for our clients requires hard work, dedication, and passion. Despite the lack of resources, we do what we can to provide the best representation for our clients.

I began to reach out to my supervisors to let them know that I wanted to take on more responsibility but was met with resistance. When my supervisors did not recognize my potential, I knew I had to take matters into my own hands. With my passion and newly acquired master's degree, I had the drive to incorporate social work into my everyday practice. Even when I was met with roadblocks, I persisted. When the opportunity finally presented itself, I took it head-on and excelled beyond expectations. One lesson that I learned was that when you develop an identity within an office, it becomes difficult for people, specifically in the supervisory positions, to view you any different than what you were, even after improving yourself exponentially. Even after proving it to them over and over, you may have to come to the realization that they may never be able to see your growth.

I dove into the world of mitigation specialist work, determined to make a difference in the criminal justice system. With no formal training available, I relied on my education and previous experience to guide me. My innovative techniques and approaches breathed new life into the cases I worked on, and the attorneys took notice. Once given the opportunity to co-chair on capital criminal cases, I realized that others in the field were hesitant to share their knowledge. I refused to let that stop me from pursuing my goals. I reached out to others and gathered as much information as I could, determined to expand my skill set and knowledge. That endless pursuit for knowledge gave me comfort and when utilized in my cases, it gave me positive results. The sweat equity that I accumulated over time, created a level of trust with the attorneys and members of the defense team. More importantly it created trust with my clients and their family.

Now, I am dedicated to helping others who may be in the same professional position I once was. I have written this part of the book on mitigation and career development hoping to guide others towards their goals and give them the support and guidance they need. I want to inspire others to never give up on their dreams and to pursue their passions with fervor. I do understand that there are others who are in search of support or guidance from a mentor but are unable to find one. I want this book to be like the cookbook for mitigation work, to help propel you forward so you could grab the wheel and steer it in the direction that you want to head in.

The defense team in a criminal case, especially in death penalty cases, is crucial to ensure that the accused has a fair trial and a just outcome. The American Bar Association has set guidelines for the appointment and performance of defense counsel in such cases. According to these guidelines, the defense team should have no fewer than two qualified attorneys, an investigator, and a mitigation specialist. The role of a mitigation specialist is particularly important in a criminal defense team. The mitigation specialist works to identify and gather evidence that can help to mitigate the defendant's culpability and reduce the severity of the sentence. Mitigation specialists often have backgrounds in social science fields such as criminology, criminal justice, psychology, sociology, and social work. A master's degree in social work and experience in felony and capital criminal cases are typically required.

The most common way to gain experience in this field is through internships. One can intern directly under a professional mitigation specialist, a private attorney, a law office, the prosecutor's office, or law enforcement. However, interning at a public defender's office is recommended. It is also suggested to have field experience as an investigator to understand the basic skill set required to investigate criminal cases.

While there are not any licensing or certification requirements for mitigation specialists, it is important to build a reputation and skill set by taking training courses and working with professionals in the field. The profession has been growing over the years, and mitigation has become a tool not only for capital criminal cases but also for promoting justice in criminal cases at all levels

There are organizations that provide training and ethical standards. The Certified Criminal Defense Investigation Training Counsel (CCDITC) is a board-certified training program that offers many training courses on various investigative techniques and mitigation specialist exercises. I'm currently a board-certified member and I find the courses to be valuable. The National Alliance of Sentencing Advocates and Mitigation Specialists (NASAMS), is a section of the National Legal Aid & Defender Association. They are dedicated to promoting fair, humane, and equitable sentencing and confinement decisions for all people in America. (www.nasams.org) They advance the field of sentencing advocacy by fostering the professional development of its members and upholding the ethical standards of practice of the organization. I also prepare presentations and provide hands-on training at the collegiate level for professional development, continuing education credits, and people who are generally interested in the field.

In a perfect world, every accused person would have access to a defense team that includes a mitigation specialist, regardless of the level of the case. The importance of mitigation cannot be overstated, and it is essential in ensuring that justice is served fairly.

However, in the real world, there are not yet enough mitigation specialists to fulfill the needs of every accused person charged with a crime. While the legal field would benefit from having more mitigation specialists who could perform all the duties listed in the ABA guidelines, this is not yet the case. Many people have never even heard of mitigation, and as a result, they may not receive the full benefits of a mitigation specialist's expertise.

It is important to spread awareness about the role of mitigation specialists in the legal field. By doing so, more people can understand the value of having a mitigation specialist on their defense team and can make informed decisions about their legal representation. Information about mitigation should be readily accessible, and it is essential to educate the public about this specialty. Ideally, all defense teams, including those at the public defender's office, would have access to a mitigation specialist on any and all levels of cases.

MITIGATION...WHY IS IT SO IMPORTANT

Mitigation is a crucial aspect of the justice system that is often overlooked. It is imperative that everyone, including defendants, their families, and members of the defense team fully understand the concept of mitigation and its importance in criminal cases. Parents should talk to their children about mitigation, and it should be a common topic of discussion amongst family members and friends, just like other social justice issues. Defendants and their families should familiarize themselves with mitigation because it can have a significant impact on their case. In unfortunate circumstances where a family member or friend is arrested, it is important to understand that they will be punished to the fullest extent of the law, particularly if they are poor and from a minority group. It is crucial to hope that the judge will have some compassion and make a judgment based on the unique circumstances of the accused, as everyone's upbringing is different. However, the judge only knows what has been presented in court, and that is usually only the elements related to the criminal conduct.

Mitigation is the process of gathering and presenting evidence to the court that sheds light on the defendant's unique circumstances, such as their background, history, and mental state. A mitigation specialist is an expert who works with the defense team to identify and investigate these factors, and present them to the court in a compelling way. The goal of mitigation is to humanize the defendant and help the judge see them as more than just their criminal conduct. It can be used to argue for a reduced sentence or a more lenient punishment.

CHAPTER EIGHT:

THE ROLE OF A MITIGATION SPECIALIST

A mitigation specialist plays a critical role on a criminal defense team. They are trained to thoroughly analyze a client's life circumstances and identify the positive and negative factors that may have influenced their behavior. This includes a review of the evidence and communication with various stakeholders, such as the defense team and the defendant's family. The mitigation specialist can assist in creating a comprehensive defense strategy for trial, sentencing, or the post-conviction stage. It is important to recognize that each case is unique and requires a tailored approach, and an experienced mitigation specialist understands this. Additionally, mitigation specialists possess varying levels of experience and expertise, bringing their unique skills and knowledge to the defense team. Their work is invaluable in ensuring a fair and just outcome for the defendant.

In a just world, we would all be given second chances to learn from our mistakes and make things right. However, the criminal justice system in our imperfect world is designed to punish rather than restore. The focus is often solely on the crime committed and not the person behind it, leaving the victim and offender in a state of limbo. It is time for a change.

Mitigation specialists play a critical role in ensuring that each person is seen as an individual and not just a case file. They have the skills and expertise to analyze a client's life circumstances, identify risk factors, and develop a defense strategy tailored to their unique situation. They work closely with the defense team to review and examine discovery, provide various viewpoints, and help the client navigate through the trial, sentencing, or post-conviction stages.

Let's take the example of the miniseries *The Night Of*. The defense attorney skillfully used mitigation to persuade the prosecutor to dismiss the case or lower the sentence. He highlighted the defendant's character and achievements, like being a straight-A student and the oldest of five children, planning to go to college. The defense attorney also showed how a simple drug possession charge could derail the defendant's progress. The defense attorney's efforts resulted in the prosecutor agreeing to dismiss the charges if the defendant committed to several hours of community service.

We need more mitigation specialists in every criminal case to help judges understand the person behind the crime, their life circumstances, and the impact of their actions on both the victim and defendant's families. In a more just world, restorative justice would be the norm, where offenders have a chance to make things right, and victims can find closure. A world where we learn from our mistakes and grow as individuals, rather than being defined by our worst decisions.

Imagine being judged based on the worst decisions you have ever made in your life? How would that feel? This is exactly what it feels like going through the criminal justice system. It is a punitive system that focuses solely on punishment and diminishes the importance of making the victim whole again. It strays from rehabilitating the person who committed the crime and does not consider the family impacted on both the victim and defendant's side. Everyday people like you and I, who are going through the lowest moments in our lives, are being judged by a judge, who knows nothing more than the criminal acts referenced on a piece of paper. They do not know anything about the person's upbringing, accomplishments, or current life circumstances. They essentially decide whether the person would be a candidate for probation, jail, or prison.

The use of mitigation in the criminal justice system is often overlooked, but certain segments of society use it regularly to minimize their risk and sentence length. This disparity in access to mitigation creates an unequal justice system, where wealthy individuals can utilize the benefits of mitigation while poor people and minorities are often left without that option. This systemic inequality is just one example of the racial injustice that is present in our justice system. My goal is to educate and empower the community on the benefits of mitigation and challenge the multi-tiered justice system that disproportionately affects black and brown people. Everyone should have access to mitigation, regardless of their race or socioeconomic status, and it is important that we work towards promoting equity in the courtroom.

Mitigation can be incredibly effective in criminal defense. Even a basic form of mitigation, such as presenting mitigating factors to a prosecutor, can sometimes lead to charges being dropped or reduced before a hearing even takes place. While this is not always the case, mitigation at any stage of a criminal proceeding can be helpful for the defendant. Mitigation can help make the defendant relatable and humanize their situation, which can create empathy and understanding among those involved in the case.

It is important to discuss mitigation strategies with your defense team early on in the case. With the right strategies, mitigation can be used both at the beginning stages of a case and later on down the line. An experienced attorney can help you understand the best approach to take based on the circumstances of your case. By using mitigation effectively, you may be able to achieve a more favorable outcome in court.

Why is mitigation vital to have in all criminal cases?
The Pew Research Center (2019) analyzed recent statistical data on criminal defendants who opted to take their cases to trial, and the results highlight the crucial role mitigation plays in criminal cases. The statistics indicate that 90 percent of criminal cases plead guilty, while only 2 percent go to trial, and out of those 2percent a staggering 83 percent are found guilty. This means that less than 1 percent of cases go to trial and win. *(See diagram below.)*

Trials are rare in the federal criminal justice system, and when they happen, most end in convictions

% of federal criminal defendants who _____ in fiscal 2018

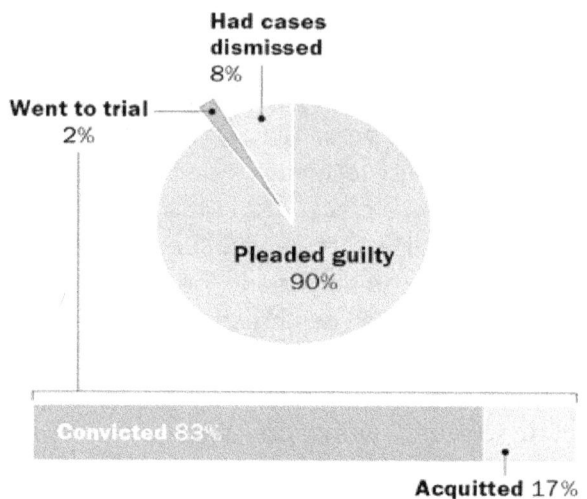

Source: Administrative Office of the U.S. Courts.

PEW RESEARCH CENTER

It is important to note that individuals who exercise their right to trial and lose could face a much higher sentence, commonly referred to as the trial penalty. Based on these figures, it is clear that the majority of cases, approximately 91.5 percent, require mitigation, as a judge will ultimately determine the sentence to resolve the case. Thus, mitigation becomes a vital part of a criminal defense strategy, as it can help negotiate with prosecutors and persuade the judge to understand the client's circumstances in hopes of receiving the most appropriate sentence. The numbers alone demonstrate how vital mitigation is for the criminal defense practice which should never be overlooked.

CHAPTER NINE:

HOW MITIGATION IS USED

ESTABLISH A THEORY

Establishing a theory as early as possible is crucial for effective mitigation in criminal defense cases. The defense mitigation theory serves as a framework to connect the client's social history and provide an explanation for their actions, without justifying the crime. It is essential to establish this theory early on in the process to test and strengthen its validity. The theory should be treated like a hypothesis in a scientific experiment, constantly challenged by evidence uncovered from witness interviews and related records. This continuous testing helps validate the premise of the theory or leads to a better theory that can be argued in court.

Starting early is the best practice, as it allows time to collect necessary records, identify and seek out witnesses, and craft detailed timelines with mitigating facts. By conducting a biopsychosocial interview with the client, a theory will naturally emerge, and the defense team can use this as a foundation for their case. Waiting too long to establish a theory can limit the effectiveness of the defense and limit the amount of time available to gather critical evidence.

When I initially receive a case, I review the discovery, preferably in its entirety. I then schedule an appointment to meet with the client to conduct a biopsychosocial interview with them. A biopsychosocial is an assessment that is typically conducted in the mental health field, which gathers information of the client's biological, psychological, and social factors. These factors are assessed to determine what is contributing to the client's presenting issues. In the field of mitigation, a biopsychosocial helps to identify a theory as to what contributed to the client's story that may have led them to be charged with a crime.

For example: In a drug conspiracy case where a client is arrested while delivering drugs, it is essential to establish a strong defense mitigation theory to explain the client's actions. During the biopsychosocial interview with the client, it is important to gather information about the client's upbringing and history of drug use. In this case, the client's parents were drug users, exposing the client to drugs at a young age and leading to early drug use. Despite attempts at treatment, the client had a long history of addiction, including previous arrests for drug possession. A possible mitigation theory for this case may be that the client's addiction and difficult upbringing led to the client's involvement in drug delivery.

Below are possible mitigation theories for similar cases:

- Clients with addiction often attempt to stay in close proximity to drugs to support their habit, and the delivery of drugs provides an opportunity to earn money to continue using.
- In many cases, clients are not the owner of the drugs and are only in possession of them for a short time.
- The amount of money gained from conducting the transaction is usually not much but enough to support the client's drug addiction.
- Sometimes clients get paid to conduct the transaction with drugs to support their addiction.

As previously mentioned, it is crucial to establish a strong defense theory early in the process to provide a comprehensive explanation for the client's actions and not justify the crime. By collecting records, identifying and seeking out witnesses, crafting detailed timelines, and utilizing experts to test and explore the theory, the defense team can build a strong case for their client.

NOW HOW DO WE SUBSTANTIATE THESE THEORIES?

When developing a mitigation theory in criminal defense, it is important to substantiate the theory with reliable evidence. This evidence can be used to support or contest the theory and help the defense team build a strong case for their client. Here are some ways to substantiate the theories developed for mitigation in criminal defense:

1. **Request Rehabilitation Records**

   Requesting rehabilitation records to show that the client was seeking treatment is supportive evidence. This can demonstrate that the client was aware of their addiction and was taking steps to address it.

2. **Obtain Jail Medical Records**

   Requesting jail medical records from the client's various arrests in the past may unveil that the client was sent to the detox unit at the jail for treatment. This can provide evidence of the client's history of addiction and efforts to overcome it.

3. **Interview Family or Close Friends**

   Interviewing family or close friends can provide insight into the client's character and the effects of addiction on the client's life. This can help to illustrate the "Dr. Jekyll and Mr. Hyde" effect of addiction and show how it affected the client's decision-making.

4. **Consult with Addiction Experts**

   Consulting with an addiction expert to conduct a psychological and chemical dependency evaluation on the client can show the long-term and short-term effects of addiction on the client's life. This can help to build a strong case for the client and demonstrate that their addiction was a significant factor in their behavior.

By using these methods to gather supporting data, the defense team can strengthen their mitigation theory and present a more compelling case to the judge. This can ultimately help to secure a better sentencing choice for the client, taking into account their unique circumstances and history.

Mental health and substance abuse are two issues that are often overlooked in our society, but they are critical issues that require our attention. Unfortunately, jails and prisons have become the largest providers of mental health and addiction services to poor individuals who experience serious substance abuse and mental illnesses in the United States. In fact, it is usually the first place they ever receive any treatment of any sort. This is unacceptable, and we must take action to make a change.

We need to understand that these individuals are not criminals; they are sick and require treatment. The first step towards change is to recognize that mental health and substance abuse issues are serious and require immediate attention. Early detection and assessment of these disorders can prevent harm to the client, inmates, staff, and later on people in the community once they are released. Restorative justice is the key to treating this societal problem. We need to shift our focus from punishment to rehabilitation and treatment.

The client should not be released from jail or prison in worse condition than when they arrived, even though this commonly occurs. We must ensure that the appropriate and viable discharge plan is in place, which promotes their well-being and supports their re-entry into society. Treatment, along with other services, should be outlined in the mitigation packet. The lack of appropriate treatment not only harms the individual but also the community as a whole. We must ensure that these individuals receive the necessary treatment and support to help them recover and lead healthy and productive lives. We can achieve this by working together and advocating for policies that prioritize mental health and substance abuse treatment as part of the criminal justice system.

It is unacceptable that jails and prisons only provide psychotropic medications for mental health and lack the necessary psychother- apy, counseling, or any coordination for inmates returning to the community. This issue is not only inhumane but also a serious threat to public safety. Inmates who suffer from mental health conditions are often released back into the community with no treatment or plan for their rehabilitation, leading to higher recidivism rates and increased risk of harm to themselves and others. We must push for reform in our criminal justice system and demand that treatment for inmates who have mental health issues become a priority. As citizens, we have a responsibility to advocate for the basic human rights of those who are deprived of their liberty. The landmark case of Estelle v. Gamble made it clear that it is the government's responsibility to provide basic health care for all prisoners. In 1977, Bowring v. Godwin extended those rights to include psychiatric care, and Ruiz v. Estelle in 1980 established minimal standards for the provision of "adequate" mental health care to inmates with mental issues. However, despite these legal precedents, we are still falling short as a society.

We must demand that education, rehabilitation, and restoration become standard practices in our jail and prison system. It is time for us to recognize that mental health and substance abuse are serious issues that require a restorative justice perspective. We need to pri- oritize early detection and assessment of these disorders to prevent harm to inmates, staff, and the community. A lack of appropriate discharge planning and viable aftercare options could be harmful to the client and increase the likelihood of recidivism. It is time for us to come together and demand change for a better future.

Mitigation in criminal defense supports these principles and is an essential component of restorative justice. Restorative justice aims to repair the harm caused by crime and to restore relationships between victims, offenders, and communities. The focus is not just on punishing the offender but also on addressing the underlying issues that led to the offense, such as addiction, mental health issues, poverty, or trauma. Mitigation helps to bring about a more restorative approach to justice by recognizing the humanity of the offender and that they are more than just the crime they committed. It takes into account the individual circumstances that led to the offense, such as addiction, mental illness, poverty, or trauma, and seeks to address those issues to prevent future offending. By addressing the underlying issues, mitigation can also reduce the likelihood of reoffending and promote rehabilitation. (Roberts, 2007)

Mitigation recognizes that punishment alone does not necessarily lead to healing or restoration. By addressing the underlying issues and providing support and resources for rehabilitation, mitigation can help to promote healing and reconciliation. Mitigation is one of the pillars of restorative justice as it seeks to address the root causes of crime and promotes rehabilitation and restoration.

CASE EXAMPLES ON DRUG OFFENSES

Mitigation is a crucial aspect of criminal defense cases where a defendant's circumstances or mental state are taken into consideration to reduce the severity of their sentence. Let's explore some real-life examples of how mitigation works in drug-related cases.

- In one case, a defendant was charged with drug possession and sale. However, upon investigation, it was discovered that the defendant had recently lost a child, which led to depression and subsequent drug use to cope with their grief. Research has shown that drug use can alter a person's cognitive functioning, and in this case, the defendant's drug use was a result of their underlying mental health struggles. This information would be presented as a mitigating factor in court to reduce the severity of the defendant's sentence.

- In another scenario, defendants who are arrested for large amounts of drugs are often not the masterminds behind the drug operation. Instead, they are often drug-addicted users who are willing to follow the orders of drug dealers to earn money to support their addiction. This argument is a mitigation theory that conveys the defendant's acceptance of their culpability in the crime while highlighting their lesser role in the overall operation.

- In some cases, defendants have experienced significant trauma in their lives, which they cope with through chronic drug or alcohol use. They may also try to stay in close proximity to drugs to support their addiction. These individuals are not typically interested in selling or distributing drugs but are instead focused on managing their addiction. This information is presented as a mitigation factor to reduce the severity of the defendant's sentence.

- In some cases, drug addiction can cause severe withdrawal symptoms, leading to chronic drug use or micro-dosing. These defendants require specialized assistance to detox safely and avoid chronic pain or even death. It is not uncommon for them to be found in possession of large amounts of drugs that do not belong to them as they may have been paid in drugs to deliver them. This scenario would fall under the mental health mitigation theory, requiring experts to examine and analyze all the evidence and medical records to provide evidence that the defendant's drug use is a result of their mental health struggles.

There are various plausible theories that offer explanations based on the client's experiences, connecting them to the instant criminal offense. In the eyes of the court, these individuals may appear as though they have no desire to follow the law, instead, spending their days using drugs, drinking, and spreading toxic chemicals throughout the community. Their actions seem to further the addiction epidemic and indirectly put the lives of others in danger. However, upon peeling back the layers, one can see the difficult circumstances that the client faced. A mitigation theory can focus on how the client's behavior is a product of learned experiences from their environment. If the client had proper tools and support, the criminal offense could have been avoided. In fact, if provided with these resources during the disposition of the client's case, they could have the opportunity to make positive changes for themselves and their community

CHAPTER TEN:

THE FOUNDATION OF MITIGATION

It is essential to build a foundation of trust and honesty to gain insight into the client's life, character, and experiences. By building a relationship with the client, the defense team can gain a deeper understanding of the events leading up to the crime and the factors that may have contributed to it. Being open and honest with the client and allowing them to be as open and honest as possible is critical in helping to build a strong case. The attorney, investigator, and mitigation specialist should make an effort to listen carefully to the client's story, concerns, and feelings without judgment. This approach will help to create a safe space for the client to share information and build a strong working relationship with their defense team.

An actionable step to consider is to meet with the client frequently. Interview the client about their life and the case periodically throughout the process. Also, it is important to establish a relationship with the client's family. In addition to building rapport with the client, it is also important to involve them actively in the case. Getting the client's opinion and including them in the direction of the case can create trust and demonstrate that the defense team values their input. By keeping the client informed and involved, they will feel empowered and have a better understanding of the process. Moreover, it is essential to follow through on promises made to the client. This could include requests for specific records or information from family members. By keeping commitments, the attorney, investigator, and mitigation specialist could gain the client's trust and build a positive working relationship. Furthermore, through the process of investigating, the defense team may uncover additional information that could lead to a deeper and greater explanation that can be used for mitigation.

FUNCTIONAL AND ACTIONABLE STEPS

A mitigation specialist possesses the necessary skills to uncover the various layers of a client's life and report the difficult struggles to the defense team. This helps to create a strategy that could help find a solution for the client. The solution may be as simple as finding relief or additional support financially, physically, mentally, socially, emotionally, or even spiritually. There are a variety of options available in the community such as family support, therapy, Alcoholics Anonymous meetings, or outpatient or inpatient substance abuse treatment, depending on the severity of the addiction.

The key is to implement restorative justice by rehabilitating the client and providing them with access to these resources. This approach reduces the likelihood of recidivism.

The United States often addresses criminal behavior through punishment as a form of deterrence. However, legislators and policymakers are starting to realize that punishment is expensive and does not necessarily deter offenders from committing further crimes. A meta-analysis report conducted by Andrews and Bonta in 2003 found a significant relationship between human service intervention and reduced recidivism rates. Offenders who received treatment had a 12 percent reduction in recidivism rates. The likelihood of recommitting a crime is further reduced if the principles of environment, risk, need, and responsivity are addressed, meaning that if a client's unique issues are taken into account, they are less likely to recommit the crime. For example, if a homeless person has access to an infinite amount of food, their likelihood of stealing food would be reduced. (*Handbook of Restorative Justice: A Global Perspective* edited by Dennis Sullivan, Larry Tifft)

To effectively use mitigation in a sentencing hearing, it is important to gather all the necessary information about the client's rehabilitation process. One essential piece of information is the treatment summary from the rehabilitation center and a certificate of completion. This shows the judge that the client is taking responsibility for their addiction problem and is actively seeking treatment. Additionally, including research and studies on the effectiveness of rehabilitation in reducing recidivism can help sway the judge's opinion.

If the client has made progress in their treatment, obtaining a character letter or testimony from their counselor can also be useful. This can be done in various ways, such as written testimony, an audio or video recording, or having the counselor appear at the sentencing hearing. Deciding which approach to take is a strategic decision that the defense team should make based on the specific circumstances of the case.

Finally, presenting acceptance into a rehabilitation program or continued treatment as alternatives to incarceration can be an effective mitigation strategy. This approach can show the judge that the client is committed to their rehabilitation and reducing the likelihood of reoffending. By gathering all of this information and presenting it strategically, the defense team can make a compelling case for mitigating the sentence and providing the client with access to necessary resources for rehabilitation.

When working with clients in criminal cases, coordinating treatment can be a powerful strategy for mitigating the consequences of the charges they are facing. To achieve the best possible outcome, it is essential to get the client into treatment as soon as possible. One approach is to start treatment at the beginning of the case, before a sentencing hearing is held. In some situations, clients may be able to receive treatment while they are in jail. However, this option may be more appropriate for clients who are released and awaiting sentencing. Completing the program and obtaining a certificate or a full treatment summary can be used in court as evidence of progress and effort towards rehabilitation.

If the jail does not allow for outsourced treatment, it is still beneficial for the client to be accepted into a treatment program. A mitigation specialist should request an acceptance letter from the program, confirming that a bed space would be available for the client upon their release. This letter could be used as part of the mitigation strategy to provide the judge with alternative sentencing options. For example, instead of being sentenced to prison, the client could be sentenced to rehabilitation. It is crucial to start treatment as soon as possible, as it shows a willingness to take responsibility for their actions and a commitment to make positive changes in their life. This approach can help the client to mitigate the consequences of their criminal charges and reduce the risk of future criminal behavior. By coordinating treatment and advocating for rehabilitation instead of incarceration, we can work to improve the client's future

What could be helpful in your quest for treatment for your client is understanding the methodology of treatment which are known as the static and dynamic factors. Static factors are things that are relatively fixed, while dynamic factors are those that change naturally over time through treatment and intervention. These factors can be used as the focal point to outlining treatment for your client. Treatment can include therapy, substance abuse treatment, and other interventions that target these specific criminogenic needs. Review the following list (Roberts, 2007).

STATIC FACTORS
- Offender's gender, race/ethnicity, age
- Offense history, previous and present convictions records
- Relationship to victim
- Trauma from childhood

DYNAMIC FACTORS
- Substance use and abuse
- Motivation
- Isolation
- Cognitive distortions
- Lack of social networks
- Lack of victim empathy
- Criminogenic needs of the offender

The Benefits of Treatment

Treatment programs provide clients with an opportunity to change their lives by addressing the root causes of their criminal behavior. These programs often offer multifaceted support that acts as a one-stop shop of resources. If you find the right program, it may even have a social worker to act as a life coach and help plan the client's future. Additionally, they may provide resources to help the client with other aspects of their life, such as finding housing or employment. These community-based agencies are often nonprofit or for-profit organizations that offer support that can have a positive effect on clients.

As a defense attorney, having a mitigation specialist on your team can be a great advantage. They can provide additional resources to aid in the attorney's arguments in court. If suitable, mitigation can be presented to the prosecutor as a negotiation tool. If you have gone through the proper channels with the prosecutor and have not seen any traction, presenting this information to the presiding judge during the sentencing hearing can be helpful. Knowing your judge and prosecutor is essential in crafting your mitigation arguments for sentencing. Some prosecutors understand individuals on a human level. Understanding what issues make them aggravated and what they are sensitive to can help you craft compelling mitigation arguments. As a member of the defense team, you want to make it easier for them to understand the client's plight and provide better options. When compelling mitigation arguments are presented, it can be challenging for them to give your client a higher sentence. This is ultimately the goal.

Essentially, treatment programs and mitigation can work hand-in-hand to create a brighter future for clients who have experienced adverse circumstances and are facing criminal charges. Presenting evidence of a client's willingness to take responsibility for their actions and make positive changes can help mitigate the consequences of their charges.

In some cases, it does not matter if the prosecutor understands the client's situation because they may require approval from their supervisors to reduce or dismiss the case based on mitigation. In these instances, the prosecutor may need some form of proof to present alongside their negotiated decision to sway their superiors. This is where a skilled mitigation specialist can be helpful. A mitigation specialist can supplement an attorney's defense argument, strategy, or presentation with a range of resources. These could include reports, photographs, videos, data, research, expert testimony, letters, or even certification of completion from treatment programs. The list of potential resources is extensive, and the mitigation specialist's ability to provide them is invaluable.

For example, imagine a client who has been charged with a drug-related offense. The defense team could work with a mitigation specialist to gather evidence that shows the client's drug use was a result of a previously undiagnosed mental health issue. They could present reports from mental health professionals, expert testimony on the link between addiction and mental health, and even certification of completion from a treatment program. This information could help the prosecutor and judge understand the client's situation better and provide more appropriate sentencing options.

Presenting mitigation in court is crucial, regardless of the results. Even if the judge does not ultimately take the mitigation into account when making their decision, it is still important for the defense team to make an attempt to present the information. This demonstrates to the client that the defense team is fighting for them and doing everything possible to get them the best outcome. The defense team must be tactful in their presentation, using the mitigative arguments to educate the court. It may take time and effort to get a breakthrough, but making the judge familiar with the issues is essential. For example, explaining generational racialized trauma and how it affected the client's environment could educate the court and impact their decision.

It is difficult for anyone to understand a client on a human level without mitigation. When a client is charged with a crime, it can be challenging for the court to see them as anything beyond a defendant. However, presenting mitigating factors can give the court a more nuanced understanding of the client as a person. Without mitigation, it is easy for the court to make assumptions about a client that are not based on the full picture. By presenting mitigation, the defense team can help the court see the client as a whole person, not just a defendant. In the end, even if the mitigation does not lead to a reduced sentence or other positive outcome, it is still important to present it. The defense team has a responsibility to do everything possible to advocate for their client and present their case in the most accurate light.

When we hear about wars in other countries, it can be difficult to empathize with those affected, especially when it feels so distant from our daily lives. We may think the criminal justice system is distant from our daily lives, but that couldn't be further from the truth. Consider this: you probably know someone who has been charged with a crime or has been a victim of one. You may even be one of those individuals. We all seek justice and the chance to grow. Mitigation provides the opportunity for both.

As mitigation specialists, it is our responsibility to make it almost impossible for judges or prosecutors to make decisions that could ruin the lives of those we represent. Whether it is a young kid, a mother of three, or an emotionally unstable and confused grandfather, we must use every tool at our disposal to ensure that they are seen as human beings with complex stories, not just criminals.

I offer this information to all levels of professionals, from attorneys and investigators to non-profit and for-profit agencies, and to anyone who wants to make a difference. Do not be afraid to utilize these unconventional but effective tools or to seek out a highly trained mitigation specialist who can help guide you in the right direction. By working together, we can help ensure that everyone is seen as a human being worthy of compassion and understanding.

CHAPTER ELEVEN

THE PROCESS OF MITIGATION

Federal criminal court is a legal system where a criminal case is brought against a person by the federal government. Once the accused individual pleads guilty or is found guilty of one or more criminal charges, the case proceeds to a sentencing hearing. This is a crucial moment in the legal process as it can greatly impact the outcome of the case. Both the defense and prosecution have an opportunity to file a sentencing memorandum, which is a document outlining the facts of the case and their position on the appropriate sentence. The sentencing memorandum is typically submitted up to a week before the actual hearing, although this can vary depending on the judge's discretion. The judge will review the materials submitted by both sides before the hearing.

Prosecutors may submit a sentencing memorandum that includes aggravating factors used to justify a higher sentence within the sentencing guidelines. In contrast, the defense would include mitigating factors along with evidence attached to the sentencing memorandum in hopes of receiving the most appropriate sentence possible. These mitigating factors can include medical and mental health records, personal and family history, and any other relevant information that may influence the judge's decision. During the sentencing hearing, both the defense and prosecution have an opportunity to present their arguments to the court. This is how the judge learns all the relevant information about the case to make an informed decision on the appropriate sentence.

Additionally, the judge considers information from the probation office, which prepares a document called the Presentence Report

(PSR). This report includes information about the accused person's current charges, criminal history, social history, and a recommended sentence. The probation office is responsible for gathering the information needed to prepare the PSR. This includes interviewing the defendant, reviewing court documents, and obtaining information from other sources such as law enforcement, family members, and employers. The probation officer may also request additional information from the defendant or other sources, such as medical or mental health records, to ensure that all relevant information is included in the report. The defense team may have another chance to provide relevant mitigating materials to the judge, through the probation department for inclusion in the PSR, which could help reduce the sentence.

Once the PSR is completed, it is provided to the judge, the prosecution, and the defense counsel. Both the prosecution and defense team would have an opportunity to review the PSR and file objections if they disagree with any of the information or recommendations included in the report. The judge would then review the final PSR along with any objections from the prosecution and defense counsel before making a sentencing decision. The judge is not bound by the probation office's recommendation, but the PSR provides important information that can inform the judge's decision-making process. The PSR serves as a guide for the judge to determine the appropriate sentence for the individual. If the judge sees that probation recognizes that the individual has a mental health condition that may have contributed to their criminal behavior, they may take that into account when determining the sentence. For example, the judge may impose a sentence that includes mental health treatment or counseling as part of the individual's rehabilitation.

Additionally, the PSR can also have an impact on the individual's Bureau of Prisons (BOP) classification. BOP is responsible for determining the facility and security level where an individual will serve their sentence. If the PSR includes relevant mitigating factors, such as mental health record or high school diploma and so on, then BOP may consider these factors when determining the appropriate facility and security level. This can potentially lead to a more appropriate placement and treatment for the individual. It also affects the conditions the individual will be subject to while incarcerated. It may not seem as important; however, an inmate's classification will make a world of a difference. The living conditions for inmates in BOP custody vary widely depending on the facility's security level. Inmates in lower-security facilities have more freedom and privileges, while those in higher-security facilities have more restrictions on their movement and activities. The BOP's goal is to ensure that inmates are housed in facilities appropriate to their security level, and they have access to educational, vocational, and other programs that will help them successfully re-enter society upon their release.

Here are the different levels of facilities in BOP:

1. **Federal Prison-Camp (FPC):** FPCs are the lowest-security level facilities operated by the BOP and are often set up as a camp. They are usually located adjacent to higher-security institutions or on the same complex. Inmates in FPCs are generally nonviolent offenders who have committed less serious crimes and have demonstrated good behavior while in custody. They are typically allowed more freedom and privileges than inmates in higher-security levels with access to outdoor recreation areas and education and vocational training programs. Living conditions in FPCs are generally considered to be more relaxed than other facilities in the BOP system.

2. **Federal Security-Low (FSL):** Low-security facilities are the next level up from FPCs and are designed for inmates who have committed nonviolent crimes and have demonstrated good behavior while in custody. Inmates in FSLs typically have more restrictions on their movement and activities than those in FPCs but still have access to outdoor recreation areas, educational programs, and vocational training. Living conditions in FSLs are still considered relatively relaxed with dormitory-style housing.

3. **Federal Correctional Institution-Medium Security (FCI-M):** Medium-security facilities are designed for inmates who have committed more serious crimes or have demonstrated poor behavior while in custody. Inmates in FCI-Ms have more restrictions on their movement and activities, and their living conditions are more structured than those in FSLs or FPCs. FCI-Ms have more cell-type housing units and fewer privileges than lower-security facilities, but they still have access to educational and vocational programs.

4. **United States Penitentiary-High Security (USP):** High-security facilities are one of the highest levels of security in the BOP system and are designed for inmates who have committed violent crimes or pose a threat to the safety of others. Inmates in USPs have the most restrictions on their movement and activities, and their living conditions are the most structured and controlled. They are housed in single or double cells, and their access to educational and vocational programs is limited.

5. **Administrative Maximum (ADX):** The ADX, also known as the supermax prison, is the highest and most secure facility in the BOP system. It is designed for the most dangerous and violent offenders. Inmates in ADXs are housed in single cells for twenty-three hours a day, and their access to the outside world is severely restricted. They have no access to outdoor recreation areas or educational or vocational programs.

Ultimately, the judge is responsible for imposing the sentence, considering all the information presented in court, in the sentencing memorandum and in the PSR. The judge's decision is final and binding. Federal criminal court is a complex legal system with multiple parties involved. Mitigation is a valuable tool that the defense should utilize to help educate the court and promote restoration on many levels of the justice system.

When preparing a sentencing memorandum, one of the most challenging aspects is determining what type of mitigation to include. The goal is to provide information that can affect the client's culpability, which can help the judge determine a fair sentence. It is important to note that the United States v. Booker decision changed the landscape of sentencing guidelines. Previously, the guidelines were mandatory, meaning that judges had to sentence defendants within a specified range. However, after the Supreme Court struck down this provision, the guidelines became advisory, giving judges more discretion to deviate from the recommended range. With this newfound discretion, judges can consider various factors when determining an appropriate sentence, including the "nature and circumstances of the offense" and the "history and characteristics" of the client. These two factors serve as the core of mitigation in criminal cases and can be crucial in influencing the judge's decision. A well-crafted sentencing memorandum that includes effective mitigation can make a significant difference in the outcome of a case.

Mitigation can be divided into two main categories: offense mitigation and personal mitigation. Offense mitigation is focused on the "nature and circumstances" of the crime itself, including any mitigating factors that may relate to the offense. These factors may be discovered through careful examination of the case, including interviewing witnesses and reviewing the discovery documents. Common examples of offense mitigation factors include the following:

- Voluntary disclosure of the offense
- Minor role arguments
- The defendant's role in the offense
- The role of others in the offense,
- The defendant's mental state at the time of the offense
- Whether the crime was a violent offense
- The effects of the offense on the community
- The drug weight involved in the crime
- Victim's forgiveness
- Whether the offense was committed to avoid greater harm.

Personal mitigation, on the other hand, is focused on the "history and characteristics" of the individual involved in the crime. These factors are known as the Booker § 3553 factors and include a range of issues related to the individual's background and personal history. For example, some of the factors that may be considered in personal mitigation include the following

- Individual's age
- Education
- Vocational skills
- Criminal history
- Traumatic childhood experiences
- Addiction
- Mental health issues
- Diminished capacity
- Medical illnesses
- Employment history
- Military service
- Acts of kindness
- Behavior after the alleged offense (especially if the subject is not in custody)
- Whether the client has shown remorse
- Acceptance of responsibility
- Culpability
- Collateral consequences suffered by the offender or their family
- Subject's family ties and ties to the community

It is worth noting that a skilled defense attorney/team would investigate all possible avenues of mitigation and present a compelling case to the court. By combining both offense and personal mitigation strategies, a defendant may receive a more appropriate sentence, thereby reducing the severity of their punishment. Thorough preparation and a well-crafted sentencing memorandum that includes effective mitigation can make a significant difference in the outcome of a criminal case.

In the legal system, the principles and framework of a biopsychosocial report are critical components to include in a sentencing memorandum and presentation. These factors should be fused with social work principles to create a comprehensive report that can be influential in a judge's sentencing decision.

According to a study conducted by John B. Meixner Jr. called Modern Sentencing Mitigation, research shows that lengthy and robust mitigation arguments are associated with lower sentences. Mitigation arguments that are supported by concrete evidence, such as medical records or specific acts demonstrating remorse, are also associated with reduced sentences. Science-based arguments about the defendant's mental and physical health, relevant to the offense, such as addiction or mental illness, are most strongly associated with lower sentences. It is, therefore, crucial to present both offense and personal mitigation throughout the disposition of the client's case to achieve the best possible outcome.

Presenting offense mitigation allows the defense team to dispute some of the facts of the case, while explicitly allowing the client to accept full responsibility for their actions. Personal mitigation, on the other hand, focuses on the individual and pulls the judge's attention away from the actual criminal offense. It helps to demonstrate that the client has genuine remorse and respect for the court and the law. In some cases, it may be helpful for clients to write a letter to the court under the direction of the defense team, which can be included in the sentencing memorandum. This letter would allow the judge to read the client's perspective prior to the sentencing hearing and would be impactful in the client's allocution at the hearing.

Crafted into the client's letter and the sentencing memorandum should be a discharge plan, depending on the circumstances. This plan should detail the steps the client will take, once they are released from custody or once the case is disposed of. By providing a discharge plan, the judge can be assured that there is a plan set in place for the client's successful re-entry into society, which could positively influence their sentencing decision.

It is important for the defense team to be aware of personal mitigation. It is also important for the client and their family to be aware of this as well. Offense and personal mitigation are both core principles that help put the puzzle pieces together so that the judge and audience could see the image in its entirety. Imagine only having one piece of the puzzle in your hand. Based on this single piece, can you determine what the complete puzzle would look like? This scenario is similar to the judge making a determination based on one piece of information, "the criminal offense." A single puzzle piece only gives you a small glimpse into what the complete puzzle looks like. That one piece of information could only provide limited insight into the client's life. However, just like a puzzle, every piece of information is interconnected and each piece helps to build a bigger picture. As you add more pieces to the puzzle, the image becomes clearer. Similarly, as you gather mitigation you could start to form a more complete understanding of what was going on in the client's life. I do not want to diminish the puzzle piece that represents the criminal conduct; however, it is important to remember that it only provides a small part of the picture. To make a well-informed decision, it is essential to gather as much information as possible, examine all of the puzzle pieces, and carefully consider how they fit together to form a more complete understanding.

CHAPTER TWELVE:

INVESTIGATIVE ALLIES

"Investigative Allies" are people who support the investigation. Investigators can use this section of the book as a resource for their investigative needs and to teach these methods to the allies to promote fairness in the client's case. This is also a good resource for the investigative allies to get for themselves and or the client's family members. Reach one, teach one.

THE CLIENT

If an individual is facing criminal charges, it is crucial for them to work closely with their attorneys to build a strong defense. One important aspect of this defense is mitigation, which refers to the efforts made by the defendant and their attorney to reduce the severity of the punishment or sentence that may be imposed by the court.

Assisting their attorney in building a strong defense can make a significant difference in the outcome of a criminal case. This can involve providing any relevant information or evidence that may support the defendant's case, as well as being truthful and cooperative with their attorney throughout the legal proceedings.

Mitigation can be especially important in criminal cases where the defendant may face harsh penalties, such as long-term imprisonment or even the death penalty. By presenting mitigating factors to the court, such as evidence of the defendant's character, background, and circumstances, the defendant's attorney may be able to secure a more appropriate sentence or even have the charges reduced or dismissed.

In addition to working with their attorney to build a strong defense and present mitigating factors, defendants may also want to consider seeking the assistance of experts in relevant fields under the direction of the defense team. Experts such as forensic specialists, mental health professionals, or other professionals who can provide additional evidence or testimony to support the defendants case could be pivotal to the resolution of the case.

By actively working with your attorney and presenting mitigating factors to the court, defendants may be able to achieve a more appropriate outcome in their criminal case and avoid some of the harsher penalties that may be imposed by the court

FAMILY MEMBER

If you are a family member of an inmate charged with a crime, your role is valuable in his or her criminal defense. Here are some ways that family members could assist the attorney in their loved one's defense and contribute to the mitigation process.

1. **Provide Information:** Family members can provide client's attorney with any relevant information that may be helpful to the case. This could include information about the client's character from childhood to adulthood, their background, and any relevant circumstances that may help to explain their personal situation and circumstances surrounding the offense. This includes but is not limited to the client's relationship with members of his family, the positive things that he or she contributed to, employment, financial circumstances, and any other facts related to the client.

2. **Attend Court Hearings:** Family members can attend court hearings to show support for the client and to demonstrate that they are taking the case seriously. It is important for the judge to understand that the defendant has a supportive family, who will be there for the long haul, especially once he or she is released. This would assure the judge that if they

issue a lighter sentence, then the defendant's family members would likely be with the defendant once they are released and deter them from recidivating. Attending court could also help to reassure the client that they are not alone in their legal proceedings. Jail is a lonely place, which often disturbs a person's mental health. Frequent communication with family promotes mental wellness and positive decision-making.

3. **Attend Meetings:** Family members can attend meetings with the attorneys, investigators, and mitigation specialists to discuss the case and provide support to their loved one. This can help to ensure that the attorney has a full understanding of the defendant's circumstances and can present a compelling mitigation argument. This could also help ensure that the defendant is fully engaged in the process and feels supported throughout the legal proceedings. During the meetings, family members could advocate for the defendant by speaking out about their situation, raising awareness about the issues they are facing, and urging others to support them. This can help to build a sense of community around the defendant and provide additional support during a difficult time under the direction of the defense team.

4. **Gather Evidence:** Family members can help the attorney gather evidence to support mitigation. This could include documents, records, photographs, or testimony from friends, family, or other individuals who could provide insights into the defendant's character or circumstances. There are several ways to provide testimony. It could be in the form of a character letter, recorded interview or testimony at court. The defense team would determine the proper way to present the testimony to the court so it is important to actively participate and engage with them.

5. **Assist with Research:** Family members can assist the attorney with research, such as looking up case law or finding

information on potential witnesses or evidence that may be relevant to the case. This should be under the direction of the defense team.

In addition to assisting with the legal defense, family members can also provide emotional and practical support to the client during their incarceration. Here are some ways that family members can support the client:

1. **Keep in Contact:** Staying in contact with the client, whether through letters, phone calls, or visits, can help to provide a sense of connection and support during a difficult time.

2. **Provide Financial Assistance**: Family members can provide financial assistance to help the client pay for legal fees, fines, or other expenses that may arise during their legal proceedings. It is also important to consider that the calorie serving amount for meals in federal correctional facilities is from 2,500 -2800 calories (for male clients) and 1800 -2000 calories (for female clients). This diet is not enough to sustain a healthy lifestyle so the demand for clients to purchase additional food and other necessities is significantly vital. Adding money to their canteen could be life-changing.

3. **Advocate for the Client**: Family members can advocate for the client by speaking out about their situation, raising awareness about the issues they are facing, and urging others to support them.

4. **Provide Emotional Support:** Family members can provide emotional support to the client by listening to them, offering encouragement and reassurance, and helping them to stay positive and hopeful throughout their legal proceedings.

STUDENTS

It is important for students to learn about mitigation in a criminal case because it helps to provide a comprehensive understanding of the criminal justice system and the factors that are taken into consideration when determining a defendant's sentence or punishment. Mitigation refers to the efforts made by the defendant and their attorney to reduce the severity of the punishment or sentence that may be imposed by the court.

By learning about mitigation, students can gain insight into the complex and often subjective nature of the criminal justice system, including the role of judges, prosecutors, and defense attorneys in the process. They can also gain a deeper understanding of the factors that are taken into consideration when determining a defendant's sentence or punishment, including the defendant's background, character, and circumstances surrounding the offense.

Furthermore, understanding mitigation can help students to develop critical-thinking skills and empathy towards those who have been involved in the criminal justice system. They can learn to evaluate the effectiveness of mitigation strategies and the fairness of the criminal justice system as a whole. Overall, learning about mitigation in a criminal case can help students better understand the criminal justice system and encourage them to become more engaged and informed. Once they are informed citizens, they could also advocate for a fair and just criminal justice system and possibly join a profession with that mindset.

ATTORNEYS

It is important for attorneys to learn mitigation techniques because they can be critical in achieving a positive outcome for their clients in criminal cases. Mitigation refers to the efforts made by the defendant and their attorney to reduce the severity of the punishment or sentence that may be imposed by the court. Effective mitigation techniques can help to mitigate the impact of the offense and present a more complete picture of the defendant's character and circumstances.

Here are some reasons why it is important for attorneys to learn mitigation techniques:

1. **Achieving a Better Outcome**: Effective mitigation techniques can help attorneys to achieve a better outcome for their clients by reducing the severity of the punishment or sentence that may be imposed by the court. This can be especially important in cases where the defendant faces a lengthy prison sentence or other serious consequences.

2. **Present a Complete Picture:** Mitigation techniques can help attorneys to present a complete picture of the defendant's character and circumstances, including any underlying issues that may have contributed to the offense. This can help to humanize the defendant and make them more sympathetic to the court.

3. **Build a Stronger Defense:** Effective mitigation techniques can also help attorneys build a stronger defense for their clients by identifying potential weaknesses in the prosecution's case and presenting a more compelling narrative of the defendant's situation.

4. **Demonstrate Compassion:** Mitigation techniques can also demonstrate compassion and empathy towards the defendant, which can be important in building trust and rapport between the defendant and their attorney.

Learning effective mitigation techniques can help attorneys to achieve a better outcome for their clients. Every attorney in criminal defense should be skilled in this area and have access to a mitigation specialist who could provide them with some direction to these methods.

PROFESSIONALS
It is important for other professionals to learn about mitigation and its impact on the justice system because mitigation plays a critical role

in ensuring that the criminal justice system is fair, just, and effective. Effective mitigation strategies can help to ensure that the punishment is proportional to the offense, taking into account the individual circumstances of the defendant.

Learning about mitigation can help other professionals to understand how the criminal justice system works and how it can be improved to ensure fairness for all defendants. By understanding the role of mitigation in the sentencing process, professionals can advocate for reforms that promote fairness and equity in the criminal justice system.

Mitigation techniques can help to promote rehabilitation and reduce recidivism by addressing underlying issues that may have contributed to the offense. Other professionals, such as social workers, mental health professionals, educators, corrections, and law enforcement could work with defendants or former defendants to provide support and resources that could help them overcome challenges and avoid future involvement in the criminal justice system. Effective mitigation requires collaboration, so it is important for other professionals who may be involved in the defendant's care and treatment to understand the goals which are restorative in nature. Learning about mitigation could help professionals to understand the importance of collaboration and teamwork in achieving positive outcomes for defendants and, in turn, society.

Learning about mitigation could also help professionals to develop empathy and understanding towards people who may have faced significant challenges and obstacles in their lives. By understanding the individual circumstances of a defendant, professionals can develop more effective strategies for supporting their rehabilitation and reintegration into society.

A NOTE FOR PROFESSIONALS

If you create something innovative during the course of your work, repeat it, analyze it, package it, and teach it. The power of innovation cannot be overstated.

It holds the key to progress, growth, and most importantly, safe-guarding the well-being of our communities. And yet, simply creating something innovative is not enough. We must take it a step further by teaching it to others. Only then can we ensure that its impact will extend beyond our own work, and reach the many individuals and groups who stand to benefit from it.

This is why I implore you to learn and practice the material presented in this book. For it is only through a collective effort to embrace these concepts and take actionable steps to implement them that we can truly make a difference in the world around us. By doing so, we will be one step closer to restoring our communities for the better and ensuring a brighter future for generations to come.

So let us not be content with simply creating something innovative. Let us go the extra mile to analyze it, package it, and teach it, so that we may unleash its full potential and make a meaningful impact in the world.

APPENDIX

CRIMINAL JUSTICE VS RESTORATIVE JUSTICE USING MITIGATION

The criminal justice system in the United States primarily operates from a punitive perspective, where the main emphasis is on punishment. This approach is evident in the prevailing trend of policies shaping our society's laws, which aim to be tough on crime. However, restorative justice offers an alternative to this punitive perspective by placing a greater focus on the restoration of our community. To illustrate how restorative justice can be implemented, the following chart presents a comparison between a case without mitigation on the left panel and a holistic approach with mitigation on the right panel. By incorporating mitigation, we aim to humanize the offender, prioritize the repair of the victim and the community, and allow space for self-improvement.

PUNITIVE JUSTICE (INVESTIGATION ONLY)	RESTORATIVE JUSTICE (INVESTIGATION & MITIGATION)
Punishment-oriented	Rehabilitation-oriented
Emphasis on the crime	Emphasis on the person
Incarceration, fines, and probation	Community service, counseling, and mediation
Adversarial process	Collaborative process
Focus on retribution and deterrence	Focus on repairing harm and restoring relationships
Little consideration for victim and offender needs	Acknowledges the needs of both the victim and offender
Example: A person who committed a crime is sentenced to serve time in prison and pay a fine	Example: A person who committed a crime participates in reparation of themselves and the community they victimized.

PUNITIVE JUSTICE (INVESTIGATION ONLY)	RESTORATIVE JUSTICE (INVESTIGATION & MITIGATION)
1 The accused bank robber is caught in the act or identified through evidence.	1 The accused bank robber is caught in the act or identified through evidence.
2 The prosecutor charges the accused bank robber with the applicable criminal offenses, such as armed robbery and assault.	2 The defense attorney investigates the accused bank robber's case and circumstances, such as their background, mental health, and other factors that may have contributed to the robbery.
3 The accused bank robber is tried in court, where the prosecutor presents evidence and argues for the accused bank robber to be found guilty and sentenced to a punishment.	3 The defense team uses a client-center approach to ensure the client had the best possible information to make an informed decision about going to trial. Ultimately, the client chooses not to go to trial and accepts responsibility for their actions.
4 The defense attorney presents a defense for the accused bank robber based on facts that they have uncovered.	4 The defense attorney presents mitigation to the prosecutor and judge at the sentencing hearing, arguing that the accused bank robber deserves a more appropriate sentence due to their circumstances
5 The judge or jury determines whether the accused bank robber is guilty or not guilty of the crimes charged	5 The prosecutor and judge may agree to a reduced sentence based on the mitigation presented.
6 If the accused bank robber is found guilty, the judge sentences them to a punishment, which may include imprisonment, fines, or other penalties.	6 The accused bank robber is sentenced to a punishment, which may be more appropriate than if mitigation had not been used.

In summary, punitive justice focuses solely on punishing the offender for the crime committed, while mitigation aims to provide a more holistic understanding of the offender's circumstances in order to obtain a just outcome in the criminal justice system.

APPLICATION OF A MITIGATION CASE EXAMPLE

Criminal Charges: Conspiracy to commit access device fraud and access device fraud

A CASE EXAMPLE WITHOUT MITIGATION

The defendant, Monica, and her boyfriend were charged with conspiring to unlawfully obtain the personal identification information (PII) of victims. Monica, employed at a Health and Wellness Center, exploited her access to clients' PII, resulting in the acquisition of thousands of victims' names, dates of birth, and social security numbers. Using an ID-making machine they owned, Monica and her boyfriend manufactured counterfeit IDs using the obtained PII. These fraudulent IDs were then utilized to fraudulently secure credit lines and open credit cards under the victims' names. Subsequently, both individuals were apprehended for their involvement in this scheme, which resulted in a total loss amounting to approximately $1,700,000.

PENALTIES:

1. Due to the loss amount surpassing $1,500,000 but not exceeding $3,500,000, the offense level was elevated.

2. Additionally, since the offense involved the possession of equipment that produced fraudulent IDs, another increment was added to the offense level.

3. Furthermore, an adjustment was made considering Monica's integral role within the conspiracy.

4. Exploiting her position at work, Monica significantly facilitated the commission of the offense by taking advantage of the trust placed in her by clients who entrusted her with their PII.

Sentencing: Considering the aforementioned scenario, Monica could face a maximum imprisonment term of five years for count one and ten years for count two. However, her guideline range of imprisonment fell between approximately forty-six to fifty-seven months. Without any mitigating factors, Monica might serve slightly over four years in prison. Notably, this would be her first experience serving a prison sentence. In contrast, her boyfriend received a sentence of eighty-one months in prison. From a punitive perspective, this scenario reflects the severity of the federal judicial system's when mitigation is not presented.

THE HEART OF THE STORY

Monica's story is a harrowing tale of a nineteen-year-old girl who faced numerous challenges and found herself entangled in the federal judicial system. Throughout high school, Monica battled weight issues and endured constant ridicule from her peers. She had always been a diligent student, consistently earning grades no lower than a B. However, her self-esteem suffered due to the persistent bullying she endured. During her senior year, Monica's life took an unexpected turn when she encountered her codefendant online on a social media website. He had deceitfully presented himself as a person her same age at the time(seventeen years old), while concealing the fact that he was actually thirty-four years old.

Monica, who had never received much attention before, found herself drawn to him. He showered her with affection and made her feel loved in a remarkably short span of time. Feeling a newfound sense of affection and acceptance, Monica, an honor roll student with a bright future ahead, made a fateful decision. She chose to move in with her boyfriend, firmly believing that she loved him. Little did she know that this decision would expose her to a world of drugs and manipulation. Her boyfriend introduced her to various substances, and although initially hesitant due to her limited experience with marijuana, Monica soon found herself addicted to methamphetamine. Her boyfriend conveniently provided her with meth whenever she desired it, leading her down a destructive path.

The relationship took a dark turn when her boyfriend's financial situation worsened. He resorted to coercing Monica into engaging in prostitution as a means to generate money for him. Monica vividly remembers the first time he proposed this idea. She mustered the courage to refuse, but her boyfriend responded with a brutal punch to her face, leaving a visible black mark under her eye. This violent act marked the beginning of Monica's entrapment in a cycle of fear and control. Her boyfriend held power over her, forcing her to comply with his demands. Whenever her boyfriend needed quick cash, he compelled Monica to participate in illegal activities.

On this fateful day, he approached her with a desperate plea, stating that he owed money to dangerous individuals and required immediate funds. He instructed her to pilfer people's personal information from her job at the Health and Wellness Center and deliver it to him. Fearful and trapped, Monica reluctantly followed his orders, unaware of the full extent of his nefarious activities. Unbeknownst to her, he exploited the victims' names to create counterfeit IDs and open fraudulent credit cards, causing significant harm to countless individuals. Monica became trapped in this cycle, obediently carrying out her boyfriend's criminal schemes, until the day her actions finally caught up with her, and she found herself in the clutches of law enforcement.

Monica's story serves as a cautionary tale, illustrating how vulnerable individuals can be manipulated and coerced into criminal activities by abusive and controlling partners. Her journey through the justice system highlights the complex and heartbreaking realities faced by those who find themselves ensnared in criminal cases, often victims of circumstances beyond their control.

MITIGATION

After learning that Monica was in the detox unit due to her addiction to methamphetamine, to support her claims, I made a request for her mental health records from the jail to provide evidence of her addiction at the time of admission.

Finally meeting with Monica, she openly admitted her addiction to meth and disclosed instances of previous visits to rehab and hospitalizations because of a drug overdose. Utilizing a client-centered approach during the biopsychosocial interview, I carefully explored the medical and mental health facilities that she was admitted into. This enabled me to create a comprehensive summary of her mental health history, allowing for a detailed examination of her level of consciousness before, during, and after the crime.

As rapport was established and trust was built, Monica revealed a crucial piece of information. Her boyfriend had introduced her to drugs, and he was her sole source of drugs. Intrigued by this revelation, I conducted a background check on the boyfriend, which uncovered a history of drug sales. Employing my exceptional investigative techniques, I inferred that Monica's boyfriend had been grooming her and deliberately used drugs to impair her decision-making abilities.

During subsequent interviews, Monica disclosed that her boyfriend had been abusive throughout their relationship. Although she had reported him to law enforcement on eight occasions, she had always refrained from pursuing charges due to fear. To strengthen our case, I submitted a public records request to obtain the police reports, witness statements, and photos related to the incidents. These records would substantiate Monica's claims of abuse and demonstrate that she had acted under duress during the commission of the instant offense.

To further support Monica's claims of abuse, I inquired about any photographic evidence. Remarkably, she had preserved photos of her injuries on her phone. Monica's mother provided a character letter that referenced the abuse that Monica experienced and the defense team used it in our sentencing presentation. Monica's mother also had possession of Monica's phone and was authorized to send me the photos of her injuries. The date stamps on each photo was invaluable in establishing a timeline of the abuse. These photographs would serve as crucial evidence during the sentencing phase.

During the course of our interview, I probed into the matter of the missing money. Monica revealed that her boyfriend instructed her to provide him with personally identifiable information (PII), in which she complied. He subsequently used this information to create fraudulent identities and credit cards, while Monica never received any financial benefit from the scheme. To gain a comprehensive understanding of Monica's financial situation, she provided copies of her bank account statements and shared relevant information. Leveraging my exceptional investigative skills, I reviewed her social media profiles to corroborate her claims, finding that her online presence aligned with her statements. I then turned my attention to her boyfriend's social media accounts, where I discovered photos of him flaunting luxury cars, expensive jewelry, and enjoying yacht rides with different women. This evidence was instrumental in presenting a compelling mitigation argument during the proceedings.

By diligently gathering records, conducting interviews, collecting photographic evidence, and employing investigative techniques, the defense team built a strong case highlighting Monica's addiction, the abusive nature of her relationship, and the financial exploitation she experienced. This comprehensive approach aimed to provide a nuanced understanding of the circumstances surrounding the crime and present compelling arguments for mitigating Monica's culpability.

NATURE AND CIRCUMSTANCES OF THE CASE USING OFFENSE MITIGATION

Offense mitigation is effective in attacking the loss amount listed in scenario one under penalties by:

- Utilizing bank account records to demonstrate that the client never received any of the funds gained from the scheme.
- Presenting images of the codefendant's lavish lifestyle to highlight that the client did not benefit financially from the illegal activities.

Offense mitigation is effective in addressing penalty #2 by:

- Establishing that the owner and sole user of the card-making device was the client's boyfriend, indicating her lack of direct involvement in the manufacturing of fraudulent cards.

Offense mitigation is effective in challenging penalty #3 by:

- Demonstrating that the client operated under duress and fear when obtaining personally identifiable information (PII) and delivering it to her abuser.
- Providing evidence (police reports, photos, and witness statements) of the abusive nature of the client's relationship to support her actions as a means of avoiding further abuse.

By leveraging these offense mitigation strategies, the defense team can weaken the prosecution's case by discrediting the loss amount attributed to the client, clarifying her limited role in the scheme, and establishing the mitigating factors of duress and fear. This approach aims to reduce the severity of penalties imposed on the client and seek a more favorable outcome in the legal proceedings.

PERSONAL MITIGATION UNDER HISTORY AND CHARACTERISTICS

Personal mitigation strategies were effectively utilized, specifically focusing on the 3553 Booker factors. The 3553 Booker factors come from the federal sentencing statute that discusses the imposition of a sentence (18 U.S.C. § 3553(a)).

Based on the Booker factors, courts should impose a sentence sufficient, but not greater than necessary to meet certain standards and to consider the factors such as, but not limited to: the need to provide restitution to any victims of the offense, nature and circumstances of this offense, the history and characteristics of the defendant, the need to avoid unwarranted sentence disparities among defendants with similar records who have been found guilty of similar conduct, etc.

The following actions were taken in the mitigation example above:

Records were utilized to illustrate the client's struggle with addiction and the impact it had on her decision-making abilities.

- Gathering and presenting evidence related to the client's addiction and drug use history.
- Obtaining records of her addiction, including instances of drug overdose and previous attempts to seek help.

Incorporating a letter from the client's mother highlighting the abuse she had endured and her efforts to overcome addiction:

- The letter provided firsthand accounts of the abuse the client had experienced, further supporting the argument of duress and its influence on her actions.

Client's determination to become sober and seek assistance from treatment facilities:

- Presenting records and letters from program facilitators.
- Obtaining letters from professionals working at the addiction program where the client received services. These letters detailed the client's progress and demonstrated her commitment to recovery.

Facilitating the client's acceptance into an addiction program specializing in abused women:

Utilizing my connections and skills as an investigator/mitigation specialist, I worked to ensure the client's enrollment in a program tailored to address the specific needs of abused women with addiction issues.

This program would provide comprehensive support and treatment, further highlighting the client's dedication to overcoming her challenges.

SENTENCE

Monica was sentenced to probation with the condition of completing the mental health program. While her codefendant/abuser/boyfriend was sentenced to eighty-one months of prison. By implementing these personal mitigation strategies, the defense team aimed to emphasize the client's addiction struggles, the abusive nature of her relationship, her efforts to seek help, and her progress in recovery. This approach sought to humanize the client, demonstrate her capacity for change, and advocate for a more appropriate sentence that would prioritize rehabilitation and support rather than strict punishment.

WORKS CITED

American Bar Association. "2008 Guideline 5.1." American Bar Association, www.americanbar.org/groups/committees/death_penalty_representation/resources/aba_guidelines/2008-supplementary-guidelines/2008-guideline-5-1/.

Annenberg Classroom. (2023). *Sixth Amendment - Right to Assistance Counsel.* Annenberg Classroom. https://www.annenberg-classroom.org/resource/right-assistance-counsel/

National Institute of Justice. (n.d.). *Wrongful Convictions.* National Institute of Justice. https://nij.ojp.gov/topics/justice-system-reform/wrongful-convictions

Moore, M., & Casabianca, S. (2022). *What is Solution Focused Brief Therapy?.* Psychcentral. https://psychcentral.com/health/solution-focused-brief-therapy

Turner, F. (1996). *Social Work Treatment 4th Ed.,* Free Press

National Association of Social Workers. (2021). NASW Code of Ethics. https://www.socialworkers.org/About/Ethics/Code-of-Ethics/Code-of-Ethics-English

Florida Department of Agriculture and Consumer Services. (n.d.). *Questions and Answers: Who is* Florida Department of Agriculture and Consumer Services

Gramlich, G. (2019). *Only 2% of federal criminal defendants went to trial in 2018, and most who did were found guilty.* Pew Research Center. https://www.pewresearch.org/short-reads/2019/06/11/

only-2-of-federal-criminal-defendants-go-to-trial-and-most-who-do-are-found-guilty/

Roberts, R. (2007). *Correction Counseling and Treatment 1st Ed.*, Pearson

ABOUT THE AUTHOR

Derrick St. Fort is a board-certified criminal defense investigator with over two decades of experience in both state and federal jurisdictions. His career is defined by meticulously tracking cases from initial charges to eventual resolution. Derrick specializes in the comprehensive assessment of each case, ensuring meticulous attention to detail while vividly and accurately conveying his clients' stories.

His pursuit of a master's degree in social work was pivotal, inspiring his role as a mitigation specialist. Derrick's extensive expertise allows him to forge empathetic connections with clients and families, humanizing the legal process and emphasizing the importance of each individual's narrative. His commitment to understanding historical, environmental, and psychological factors sets a new standard in criminal defense, ensuring thorough consideration of every client's circumstances.

As a respected board-certified criminal defense investigator, Derrick is sought after for his expertise and has contributed to the field through teaching and presenting at national conferences. His insights benefit legal professionals across the country, including attorneys and investigators, who value his innovative approaches to defense strategies. A Miami native with deep Haitian roots, Derrick is driven by a profound commitment to public service and social justice. He advocates tirelessly for marginalized communities, ensuring every client receives fair and equitable representation.